Real Irish Ghost Stories

Real Irish Ghost Stories

Paul Fennell

CURRACH
PRESS

Thanks to Jo O'Donoghue and all the team at Currach Press for believing in this project.

First published in 2009 by
CURRACH PRESS
55A Spruce Avenue, Stillorgan Industrial Park, Blackrock, County Dublin
www.currach.ie
1 3 5 4 2
Cover by Claire McVeigh
Origination by Currach Press
Printed in Ireland by ColourBooks, Baldoyle Industrial Estate, Dublin 13
ISBN :978-1-85607-986-0

This book is specially dedicated to my wife, Angie,
and my daughters, Suzanne and Mychelle

What you are now we used to be.
What we are now you will be.
Cemetery of the Capuchins, Rome

CONTENTS

INTRODUCTION

The veil between reality and the paranormal is so thin that sometimes people mistake reality for the paranormal. They sometimes mistake the paranormal for reality. During my many years as a paranormal investigator I have come upon some very strange things that could be rationally explained after a thorough investigation but I have also experienced some extraordinary occurrences for which science still has no explanation.

As children, how many times have we awoken in the middle of the night from a scary dream and been frightened by monsters under the bed or in the wardrobe? How many times have we left the light on or the door open while curled up under the blankets so that no one can see us? Now that we have 'grown up' and dismissed those childish fantasies and vivid imaginings of night time, do we look back and wonder why we felt that way?

My introduction into the world of the paranormal started at a very young age. This is my story.

I was born in 1964 in a Corporation house in an area called Crumlin on the south side of Dublin. I am the youngest in a family of five brothers and two sisters. Shortly after I was born my mother was told that I had pneumonia. She was advised to enjoy the short time she would have with me as I had only a few weeks to live. One evening when I was just three months old I was lying in my cot in the front room of my family home. Around me were my brothers and sisters. My mother was in the kitchen preparing the evening meal to have ready for my father when he returned from work.

My family's account of what happened next is as follows. There was a knock on the door. One of my brothers answered the door and standing there was a monk dressed in brown and cream clothing with a thick rope tied around his waist. He brushed my brother aside and walked into the house and straight over to my cot. Standing over me he proceeded to bless me and touched my forehead with his hand. My brothers and sisters let out a scream to alert my mother that a stranger was in the house and at my cot. She ran in from the kitchen just as he was leaving the house through the front door. She followed him out towards the door demanding, 'Who are you and what are you doing in my house?' She walked out into the street after him but he had vanished. My mother searched down the side of the house and up and down the street but he was gone. Because of the way my house was situated there was no possible way for anyone to disappear or hide without being seen. Who this monk was or where he came from no one knows. One thing is for certain: I survived the pneumonia and I am now married with a beautiful wife and two beautiful daughters. I am ever-grateful to whoever this monk was. I have searched for the answer to this mystery but have not found it yet.

Paranormal happenings did not visit me again until I was in my early teens. I was asleep in bed one night when I was woken by the sensation of someone sitting on the end of my bed. My bedroom was always illuminated because there was a street lamp just outside my house. I looked at the end of my bed, expecting to see my mother or one of my brothers with whom I shared my room, but none of them were there. What I did see was a person's black cloud-like figure. I could not make out if it was male or female. I just knew it was there and facing me. My knees shot up into my chest and as I pulled them in harder I could hear and feel my heart pounding. I tried to let out a scream but could only make the sound in my mind; such was my fear that nothing could come out of my mouth. I stayed like this for about ten minutes until I started to think that if the figure wanted to hurt me it would have done so by now. So I began to relax a little but kept a fixed stare on the figure sitting on my bed.

After what felt like an eternity the figure raised itself from my bed. I could feel the end of my bed lift as the figure moved up into a standing position. The figure continued to look at me for a few more seconds until it turned and just dissipated into nothing. I did not sleep a wink all night, wondering if it would return. I did not tell any of my family about this in case they thought that Paul had flipped.

From that day on the happenings in my mother's house became more frequent. These manifestations included the temperature dropping in a room in the middle of a hot summer's day and a dark shadow passing by the open door of my bedroom. When I called out to ask if anyone was there, silence was my only reply. Often I would be coming down the stairs and would hear a female voice call my name in a whisper, knowing that at the time I was alone in the house. The shock of this caused me to take the full flight of stairs in one step. The spirit presence in my mother's house continued to make itself felt until I eventually got married and left home. This has continued to the present day. Thankfully the experience left me with a great interest in and respect for the paranormal and the spirit world. I feel too that at different times during my life the presence of the monk is still with me. I believe this because a couple of times in my life I was in danger and something intervened in the situation, allowing me to come safely out of it.

Deep in my mind I wanted to know the meaning of these occurrences. Why was I experiencing them and who was causing them to happen? This led me to become a paranormal investigator, researching into the spirit world here in Ireland. Little did I know that this decision would take me into one of the most fascinating and interesting worlds you could ever imagine. During my years as a paranormal investigator I have experienced many strange encounters for which I use the phrase 'from the other side'. These include hearing a female crying from an empty room and hearing footsteps coming past me on a staircase. I have also investigated countless properties with all sorts of spirit activity, ranging from a simple playful spirit to a very nasty poltergeist that terrorised and drove a family from their home. I have even had the pleasure of spending a night locked up in Ireland's most haunted jail, Wicklow Gaol. (I must add that this jail is now a museum.) This night was by far the most eventful of all my years as a paranormal investigator.

My most significant experiences during the years were

the thousands of stories people told me about happenings involving their loved ones coming back to them time and time again. I always love listening to these fascinating stories because they are at the heart of the paranormal world. They are very important to the people telling them. Some are easy for them to tell as they are quite funny experiences; others are emotionally heart-wrenching accounts of lost loved ones. Every time I sit down to listen to these people they all seem to ask me the same question, 'Am I going mad or are these things real?' This is a very difficult question to answer off the cuff. First I have to look closely at the person in question. Are they suffering from a serious bereavement? Was it very recent and what is their state of mind at the moment? People who are experiencing this sort of bereavement can interpret simple everyday experiences as evidence that their loved ones are trying to make contact with them. This is a perfectly natural experience to have after such a huge and terrible loss. In these cases I usually comfort them and express my sadness at their loss but I do keep in contact with them. I would never tell them that the event is probably just a figment of their imagination as each person must be allowed to go through the grieving process in his or her own way.

The stories that continue to fascinate me are those that concern happenings when the people are over the grieving process and are not thinking about their loved ones. Some experience visitations if they were not present at the time of their loved ones' passing over and those who have passed on come back to say goodbye as they leave their earth life for the spirit life. These are cases where people's minds are not playing tricks on them or affected by wishful thinking;

in my opinion these are real encounters with the spirit world. They are stories that will make the hairs on your neck stand up and touch every raw emotion in your heart. Some will make you sad; others will put a peaceful smile on your face as you remember your own loved ones who have passed away.

The accounts were given to me by people who have been touched in this special way from far beyond the grave by their loved ones in the spirit world. When I first started to write down these beautiful accounts I used my own words but I felt I was somehow taking away from the raw emotion that the storytellers were experiencing as they put pen to paper to tell their story. So I present them here without editing, allowing the people who experienced these occurrences to tell their own story.

At the request of the storytellers I have changed their names and locations. This is to protect some family members that were hesitant about their stories being told and because some were afraid it would affect the future sale of their property. You know who you are from your stories and experiences and I thank you for allowing me the opportunity to tell them here.

What Haunts Us?

Before we go into the world of ghostly visitations and sightings it is important to understand what these people experienced and just what was happening in their life. So, what haunts us? To the ordinary person all paranormal visitations come under the one heading of 'ghost'. But just what are ghosts and are they real?

A ghost is just residual energy; this is the term by which it is scientifically known. Residual energy is a playback of a past event. The apparitions in question were once living people and have left an impression in time within some location. They are recordings of an event captured by the structure of the building.

There are numerous theories about how these residual hauntings come to be. The main theory is that they are like a video playback. As you know, video and audiotapes capture sounds and images using a special material that is oxidized. Certain building materials, such as slate and stone and some iron nails used in many older buildings have been found to have a similar oxidized material in them, making it possible for the building to record events in its structure.

The materials store the energy created by certain joyful or traumatic events and play them back at a later time. We are not sure what causes the playback of these events; this remains a mystery to us today. Sometimes it can be as simple as some construction work or renovations being carried out on the location that triggers off the playback. One thing you must remember is that these ghostly apparitions are only a playback; they are not spirits and cannot see you. These apparitions cannot interact with you or harm you in any way. Even though you can see and hear them it's just like being at the movies. They might scare you but they cannot harm you.

Also included under the general heading of 'ghost' is the more fascinating world of spirits. Within this world you have spirits that are grounded or that come in visitation. They can be crisis spirits or poltergeists or, the most terrifying and feared spiritual happenings, demonic possessions. But what exactly do all these terms mean? What makes each one so special that they stand out on their own?

Grounded Spirits
A grounded spirit is a spirit that has become trapped within the confines of a building or place. It may be the spirit of a person who has died and for some reason either does not know how to cross over to the higher plane or simply does not want to. They sometimes do not even know that they are dead and can become annoyed because they are being ignored by their loved ones. They will continue to haunt a particular location to which they feel most attached but like all spirits can move about freely and at will. Mostly the manifestations are reported soon after a sudden death of a family member and are witnessed by several people.

Grounded spirits are a little more complicated than other examples of residual energy. When you come across a 'ghost' you simply see it. You might be a little startled but you soon calm down. Now the situation has stepped up a notch: when you step into the atmosphere of a grounded spirit not only can *you* look upon it but it can turn around and look back at you and acknowledge you in its atmosphere.

Visitation Spirits
Spirits that come in visitation can easily be mistaken for grounded spirits as they, like grounded spirits, will interact with you when you enter their atmosphere. These spirits are those who have crossed over and gone through their healing process. For some reason they have decided to return to visit their loved ones or a place that was a favourite when they were living and earthbound. They can also come back to protect or reassure loved ones when the living are in danger or in need of comforting. One thing you must remember – and this will become apparent as you read the following accounts – is that if spirits were kind-hearted while earthbound, that personality will carry over with them and make them happy, kind and loving spirits. Equally important is the fact that if they were nasty people – for example violent people – while earthbound, this personality will also carry over with them into the spirit world. We are who we are and although we leave our bodies behind when we die, our souls and our personalities remain with us in the afterlife.

Crisis Spirits

Crisis spirits are the spirits of loved ones who at the time of their death visit their friends or family just to say, 'I am OK and I will see you again in the next world.' Sometimes they come to warn loved ones that they – the crisis spirits – are in grave danger. A good example of this would be a mother of a soldier serving in a war overseas either seeing her son in her house or feeling his presence near her. She might smell his aftershave or hear his favourite song on the radio. Something would happen to make her think of her son. She would then get news within the next few days that her son had been killed in action at the same date and time she felt his presence. To me crisis spirits are the most beautiful spirits you will ever encounter for they have taken the time at this point in their spiritual development to say a final goodbye to their loved ones. If you are ever touched in this way at a friend's or family member's death, remember that you must have been someone special to this spirit for them to act like this.

Poltergeists

Modern media have fuelled our imagination with weird and strange demons that enter our world through our television sets and take our children into another realm. In reality poltergeists are malevolent, mischievous forms of energy that manifest themselves in some of the following phenomena: strange noises, moving or disappearing objects and strong, abnormal odours. These are just a few examples. The word *poltergeist* is a German word meaning literally 'noisy spirit'. Why exactly poltergeist activity occurs has been the subject of great debate by experts and scientists for decades. Independent studies done on poltergeist activity have shown that the majority of cases are associated with an individual residing in the property and not the property itself. The phenomenon seems to be linked to a type of subconscious psychokinesis (PK) on the part of the individual. These individuals are usually in their early teens, especially young females entering puberty, and are totally unaware that they are involuntarily directing the poltergeist energy. Poltergeist activity usually begins and ends abruptly. An individual incident can last for several hours or several years, stopping and returning continually during this time. Poltergeist energy often attaches itself to teenagers who are suffering some sort of mental stress rooted in hardship or poor physical health. Emotional problems associated with individual personalities may be anxiety over exams, hysteria and anger over the break-up of their parents' marriage or personal obsessions. In some cases the sufferers are able to solve the problems, with psychological and professional help, and this can lead to the poltergeist energies disappearing. Other cases of poltergeist activity can be attributed to supernatural forces including demonic influences brought about by foolish dabbling in the occult and untrained participation in Ouija-board sessions.

I will try to explain how to differentiate between a poltergeist and haunted activity even though they share the same incidents of apparitions, strange noises, odours and moving or disappearing objects. There are some aspects of their activity that make them different and you must become familiar with them. Hauntings involve the spirits of deceased people that appear frequently in certain places and times. Poltergeists are not spirits at all; they are a build up of PK energy that a living person is unknowingly controlling. With hauntings, the spirits are of people known to the deceased before the time of their death. Poltergeist activity can be triggered by a living person's state of mind in any location, at any time. In the case of hauntings, activities are continuous over time and there is a history behind them. Poltergeist activity builds up over time to a climax with a sudden stop. Then the energy builds up again and the activity will start again. With hauntings, spirits usually remain at the location and do not follow anyone. In the case of poltergeists, the energies can travel anywhere with any one individual that they are attracted to.

Demonic Possession

This kind of spiritual possession involves external forces whereby certain malevolent, extra-dimensional entities or demons gain control over a person's body, which they then use for an evil or destructive purpose. The person possessed has no control over the possessing entity, so it will persist until forced to leave, usually through a form of exorcism. Exorcism is the practice of evicting demons or other evil spiritual entities which are supposed to have possessed (taken control of) a person. The practice is quite ancient and is still part of the belief system of many religions. The person performing the exorcism, known as an exorcist, is often a priest or an individual thought to be graced with special powers or skills. The exorcist may use religious material such as prayers and set formulas, gestures, symbols, icons, amulets, etc. The exorcist often invokes some benign supernatural power to perform the task.

In general, possessed people are not regarded as evil

in themselves; nor are they wholly responsible for their actions. Therefore, exorcism is generally thought of more as a cure than as a punishment. Exorcisms can also be performed on a building to rid it of demonic forces that may be attacking an individual or the family living in it.

Your Stories

ALISA, WATERFORD

My father was diagnosed with cancer and put up a good fight against it but sadly the cancer began to win the battle. My brothers and sister took turns to visit my father in hospital but my mother never left his bedside. She stayed there day and night during his last few weeks. The day my father passed away I will never ever forget. I was at home in my parents' house and I remember looking at the clock. It was just 1.45 pm. I went into the kitchen to make some lunch for myself, when I heard a sound that I knew all too well. It broke my heart because I knew what it meant. What I heard was the noise of a metal chain against the down-pipe at the side of our house. You see, my father always used a bicycle; he never drove a car – in fact he could not drive at all. We always knew when Dad was home from work as we could hear the noise of the chain on the down-pipe as he locked his bike to it. I instinctively knew that Dad was gone. I just sobbed my eyes out in the kitchen. I recall one of my brothers rushing in to see if I was OK and all I could say was, 'Dad's gone. I know he is.'

To try and calm me down he said he would ring the hospital to get some news but as he spoke to my other brother who was in the hospital I could see from his face that I was right. I guess Dad just wanted to say goodbye in his own special way. That day was the saddest day in my life but in a way I am glad he chose to do what he did because I know he did not want to leave without saying goodbye. I still hear that sound from time to time but it now brings happiness into my life for I know that Dad is around and still looking after us in his own special way.

TARA, DUBLIN

When my family lost our mother the grief and loss were hard on all of us but they affected my sister Paula more than the rest of the family. I recall this incident as if it was yesterday. It was a few months after our mother died when I received a phone call from Paula (who at the time was feeling very depressed). Paula explained to me that she had returned home from some grocery shopping and, feeling tired, she sat on the sofa still wearing her coat, which was wet from the heavy rain outside. We chatted for a while until she finally explained to me that she was sitting there thinking of Mum, naturally feeling very down within herself. Then she said, quite unexpectedly, that there was a snow-white dove outside her patio doors. There was a change in her voice as she said those words to me, as if she was more joyful. Keeping this going, as I was glad to hear her more cheerful, I said 'Ah, that's so sweet.' Paula agreed but said that she thought it was strange as it was such a dull rainy day.

Paula then paused. The phone went silent.

'Are you OK, Paula?' I asked. 'Are you still there?'

I was relieved to here her say, 'Yes. I'm here.'

'What happened? You went silent.'

Her answer shocked me. 'Tara, I think the dove at my patio door is Mum. I think it's Mum trying to tell me something.' I told Paula to ask, 'Is that you, Mum? Let me know by going over to the tree that we planted in your garden.' No sooner had she said this than the dove flew over to the tree and back to the doors. We got our answer. Paula then opened the patio door, thinking that the dove would fly away like all birds do. To her great joy the dove came into the house and flew around the dining room and the sitting room. It stayed in the house long enough for Paula to take several pictures of it sitting just in front of her Christmas tree. She then thanked Mum for letting her know she was OK. The dove then left and so did the depressive feelings Paula had been having since our mother's death. Since that day all the family know that our mum is OK wherever she is and that she is still watching over her family. Before this incident I would never have believed that spirits could return but I know that Paula would never lie to me about anything like this. I am so thankful that our family has being touched like this, that Mum is OK and happy in the afterlife.

JANET, CAMBRIDGE

My mother came to stay with me after a bout of illness. She became unwell after a few days and was admitted to hospital where she died after a week. Although she was seventy years old her death was unexpected and obviously caused shock and grief. There was much unrest within the family, and I often found myself grieving alone.

My mother had a six-year-old King Charles spaniel that she adored and I became the dog's new owner. I already had two cats that I had owned for fifteen years. About a month after this I noticed that the animals would suddenly wake up and follow the movement of something across the room or from the top to the bottom of the stairs. The dog's behaviour became more erratic with each passing day and whenever anyone was in the house she was like a shadow. The cats spent longer and longer outside and at times refused to come in even for food. As time went on the dog refused to sleep downstairs in her basket and would follow me to bed. All my attempts to calm her failed and she was turning into a nervous, frightened dog. My initial reaction was that my own unhappiness was causing the change in the animals. I believed that I was becoming more forgetful as things became misplaced in the house. When I told the story at work someone suggested that my mother might be visiting the house to make sure we were OK.

I then consulted a medium. I did not state how long before then my mother had died as I had read that spirits did not normally communicate until about six months after death. I just asked if there was anyone who had a message for me? She gave me enough details about my mother and father for me to believe she was communicating with them. She even mentioned that I had changed the colour of the bedroom my mother had slept in and gave details of her funeral. She also confirmed that my mother was indeed visiting and at times stroking the dog. No wonder she was a nervous wreck! My mother was not a believer in the afterlife and her excitement that she was with my father and able to visit was unbelievable! After further visits to the medium we managed to sort out all my mother's unresolved issues. Although I know she still visits and attempts to contact me through dreams, the animals are no longer afraid and I know that she is still trying to mother me from the other side. I have gained a great deal of comfort from this fact. I still miss and grieve for my parents but I know that they are only in the next room and still visit when I need them.

DAVE, SLIGO

When I was just eight years old my grandfather passed away. I was in school when it happened. On my way home from school that day I stopped off at Grandad's house as usual. But this time, instead of the house being empty except for Grandad it was full of people from the town. As I went inside I found my mother crying in the front room. 'Where is Grandad?' I asked, but she just hugged me and said, 'He is gone, Dave; he is gone.' That day, I lost my grandad and my friend did too as I had spent most of the time after school up in my grandfather's house playing.

At the time my parents felt that it would be best that I did not attend the funeral, as I was upset enough as it was. I recall that after his funeral our house was full of family and friends and a few people who were strangers to me. At the time I thought they were strangers but I later found out that they were family from England who had travelled over for the funeral. They sat around drinking tea and eating food prepared by my mother. I recall feeling left out, a stranger in my own home.

I went up to my room to get away from it all. I closed my bedroom door and lay on my bed thinking of Grandad, when I felt as if someone was watching me. I then became aware of a figure standing beside me. It was an old lady.

I thought this was a little strange, as I had not heard my bedroom door open. It was an old door and the handle was loose and rattled as you tried to turn it. But I was so young at the time that I thought nothing more of it. The old lady sat on the bed beside me and asked why I was so sad and not downstairs with the rest of the family. I explained to her that I was missing Grandad and just wanted to be on my own. She then said that Grandad missed me too and that he wanted me to know that he was OK and in heaven. This was the first time I ever heard his name, as he was always Grandad to me. 'How do you know Grandad?' I asked her, as I had never seen her anywhere in my town before and at the time it was a small town on the outskirts of Sligo. 'I knew your grandfather John very well, Dave. Very well.' We chatted for some time about Grandad and how I loved to play at his house after school. She cheered me up as I felt very close to Grandad that day.

Some days passed when my mother asked if I would like to come with her to Grandad's house as she needed to do some work there. She was starting to clear his place out to get it ready to sell. I helped by filling boxes and bags with Grandad's stuff. My mother stopped and said, 'Look, it's you in Grandad's old photo album.' We sat there looking at old photos of all the family. Some I knew; others I asked about. Then I saw in a picture Grandad and the old lady who had chatted to me on the day of the funeral. I asked, 'Who is she?'

My mother replied, 'That's your grandmother, Dave. You never knew your grandmother. She died long before you were born.'

'She can't be dead, Mum; she was at the funeral.'

'Don't be silly, Dave. You must be mistaken.'

'No Mum it's her. She came to me when I was upstairs. She told me that Grandad was OK and that he was in heaven. She called him John. Was that Grandad's name?' I asked.

My mother looked at me in a way I will never forget. For, as we all now believe, I was visited on that day by my grandmother, Grandad's wife, but also my mother's mother. I believe that my grandad was getting a message to me because I was not there when he passed away. I now firmly believe that he is with me all the time.

MICHAEL, DERRY

In 1978 we lost our son Josh. At the time our world was devastated – we had lost everything. But as in the old cliché, life must and will go on, even though at the time we did not want it to. In 1981 we had another son, Stephen, and thank the Lord he was a healthy boy. At the time of this story Stephen was eight years of age. He would play games around the house, up in his bedroom and out in the backyard, and like all kids of his age he had an imaginary friend he would play games with, or so we thought.

It was a bright, warm summer's day and my wife Anne was in the sitting room watching television. She could hear Stephen playing upstairs in his room. He was giggling away and she could hear him talking to his imaginary friend. Then she heard him running into the kitchen. 'What are you up to?' she enquired as all mothers do. 'I am getting a drink, one for me and one for my friend.' Now she thought he actually had a friend in playing with him, one of his friends from the street. As Stephen was going back up the stairs Anne said to him, 'Don't make a mess up there. I have just cleaned those rooms.'

Some time later, Anne was upstairs and heard Stephen having a great time playing in his room with his friend. She wanted to know who it was just in case his mother was looking for him, so she went into the room and found Stephen playing on his own. On the floor were a pile of toys and two glasses. The one beside Stephen was empty and another one across from him was still full. Still thinking that he was playing with his imaginary friend Anne asked, 'Is your friend not thirsty?

'Not yet,' Stephen said, 'but he is very happy to see you.'

'Oh! And why is that?'

'He says he misses you.' Playing along as a mother would, she said, 'How could he be missing me when we have never played before?' Stephen went silent for a while then said, 'You used to play with him but you stopped.'

'What do you mean I used to play with him?'

'He said that you played with him the way you play with me here in this room.' At this time Anne was becoming concerned with the way this situation was developing, as Stephen's room had been Josh's room when he was alive. 'So tell me, Stephen, how old is your friend?'

'He says he is ten.' Anne said her heart sank when Stephen said this for that was Josh's age when he died. She recalls that she was shaking before she asked the next question. 'So tell me, Stephen, what is your friend's name?'

'Josh. His name is Josh.' Anne grabbed Stephen and took him downstairs where she questioned him about

Josh. It turned out that for as long as he could remember Stephen had played with Josh in his bedroom and even said that Josh used to visit him at night and Stephen and he would play games.

I remember getting a phone call from Anne in work that day. She was very distressed and asked me to come home as soon as possible. When I arrived home she revealed the day's happenings. I was numb. I did not know what to do. I tried to recall if we had ever discussed Josh with Stephen to see if we had triggered anything in order for him to create this imaginary friend. But we had not. I asked Stephen to describe his friend to us and he described Josh. At the time we did not tell Stephen why we were so anxious when we found out who this friend was. Later on we did tell him who we suspected his childhood friend was.

I feel that two things came out of this incident: Anne and I knew that our first child was still with us and that he would always be with us. Josh somehow had a brother to play with, as did Stephen, even though at the time he was unaware of it. Secondly, it had a great effect on Stephen when we recounted the story of his childhood friend to him. The experience has bonded this family more strongly than anyone could ever have imagined. Even though we physically lost Josh he always remained with us spiritually.

DEREK, COUNTY DUBLIN

In 1960 I was just nineteen and serving as an apprentice in Cambridge, England. On the site was a group of lads who played around with the Ouija board. I was somewhat interested in what was going on so one day I joined in with them. Nothing was happening, not even a twitch out of the glass. I was just about to leave the table when the glass spelt out 'Freeman'. I froze, for that was my mother's name. I asked was there anyone there. The glass spelt out 'Yes.' I looked around at the rest of the lads at the table. I said, 'Guys, if you are messing it's not funny.' Then the glass spelt out. 'Yes. Larry Mullins, cousin of Deirdre.' These names I did recognise and I knew that nobody else around the table did. Then the glass spelt out, 'You must belt your mum.'

I asked, 'Why should I belt my mum?'

I was shocked at what the glass spelt out. 'She would not send me to hospital.' This meant nothing to me but obviously something happened long ago that involved someone dying and they felt they should have been sent to hospital. Then the glass spelt out, 'It's Michael, late husband to Suzanne.'

Then it spelt out, 'Tell her I still love her and you do as you are doing.' I was unsure who was talking to me at this point. Was it Michael or was it Larry? Well, I did not care. I jumped up from the table and left the area. I never used an Ouija board again.

FIONA, COUNTY CORK

It all started after a sickness hit the family. John, my youngest son, became ill. So as not to have him away from the rest of the family we made him a bed on the settee in the living room. As he lay on the settee we all noticed that the wind chime that hung above the window was moving at high speeds in all directions, clanging and rattling. This was strange: we had no windows or doors open because John was unwell and there was no draught around at all. We tried to put it out of our minds as best we could by putting it down to some wind that we could not feel and continued with our normal family life.

After that one of our daughters, Janet, went to hospital for a kidney-stone operation. When she was back at home recovering, as part of her long-term treatment for the kidney stones she had to drink a lot of water. This particular night she woke up in the middle of the night and felt very thirsty so she went down to the kitchen to get herself a glass of water. As she was filling her glass from the sink she heard her name being called. When she looked up at the window, she saw an image of an old man directly above her head. She described him as a very old man with white hair. He was looking straight at her, calling her name. We all woke up, thinking that someone had broken into the house and rushed down into the kitchen. There we found Janet standing at the sink shaking all over. She could do nothing but stare out into the back yard. My husband ran out the back thinking someone was there, but found no one. When Janet told the rest of the family what she had seen nobody believed her. We all thought it might have been a delayed effect of some medication she had taken but she was adamant that she saw this man in full consciousness.

It was not until a few days later that one of my neighbours was around for tea. I told her of the strange night we had and that I thought it was all in Janet's mind. She stopped me and told me that it might not be in her mind and went on to tell me a story the previous owner had told her. She told me they had seen a very similar man once who nearly frightened them to death. This happened when the mother of the family was putting out her rubbish bin late one night for bin collection early the next morning.

That night she saw the image of an old man at the side of the house. She shouted at him, 'Who are you?' but he did not run away – he more or less vanished into nothing. She also said that as he was vanishing he was calling out her name. This sent a huge cold shiver through my body.

I never told Janet about this as I felt it might just upset her even more. Many other inexplicable things happened in that house after that. For example, when I was in the kitchen preparing a meal I would have the radio on in the front room. All of a sudden the station would change. This would only happen when someone was alone in the house. In the height of summer you could walk into a room and it would be icy cold even though the rest of the house would be warm with no heating on. Then sometimes I might be getting dressed in front of a mirror and see someone walking past behind me but when I checked the rooms I was alone. It was when the rest of the family reported seeing and feeling all these things and not just myself and Janet that we decided enough was enough! We sold up and moved house. Since then we have had a peaceful life.

MICHELLE, COUNTY OFFALY

In June of 1997 we bought an old farmhouse in Tullamore, County Offaly. It was about a hundred and fifty years old – well, that's what the estate agent said. It did need a lot of repair but my husband was good at DIY and we always wanted to renovate an old house. We had to tear down walls and ceilings that were beyond repair and replace them. Underneath the floor covering we found old newspapers dating back to 1930.

It all started one evening. My husband worked the night

shift as a security guard. We had a teenage daughter living with us at the time so I was not left alone at night. This night I was woken from my sleep by a noise like someone strangling a cat. The sound seemed amplified. The sound resonated and then slowly became lower and softer until it finally faded away. What scared the hell out of me was that it was just outside my bedroom door. I jumped up and quickly opened the door but there was nothing there. I checked my daughter but she was sound asleep. I returned to bed but did not sleep for the remainder of the night.

Several nights later I was in the front room, watching television. My daughter had gone out with some friends and I was expecting her home later on that night. At the time I had one light on in the living room and one in the porch. I suddenly became aware that the kitchen light had been turned on. I called out, 'Is that you, love?', expecting my daughter to reply. Thinking she had not heard me I got up expecting to see her in the kitchen but nobody was there. I went to her room to see if she was there but her room was empty.

Another evening after that, my husband and I had gone to bed and my daughter was in her bedroom when suddenly she heard a loud knocking on her door. Thinking it was me, she said, 'Come in,' but the door didn't open. She got up and looked out; no one was there. She then knocked on our door and popped her head in. I was still awake and she asked if either of us had just knocked on her door. I replied, 'No. Are you sure you heard knocking?'

Then one day I was in the bathroom fixing my make-up. The door opened and I heard footsteps going by the door. I turned and caught a glimpse of what I thought was my daughter going towards the front bedroom. I turned back to the mirror and just then I heard the front door open. It was my daughter coming home from school. I rushed into all the bedrooms to see what it was that I had just seen but all were empty.

One morning as I stood at the top of the stairway I could hear the loud moaning of a female voice. This time my husband heard it. The sound seemed to be like someone who was suffering and in pain. We searched the entire house from top to bottom but found nothing.

On another occasion my daughter had just come out of the living room and saw what she thought was me walking into the kitchen. She called out and started to follow the figure into the kitchen, when all of a sudden I arrived home and came in through the hall door. My daughter's face was ashen. She started shaking saying, 'Mum, you just went into the kitchen. I was following you. I saw you.' We both rushed into the kitchen but there was nothing and there was no way for anyone to escape as the back door was locked.

Later we explained to my husband exactly what had happened that day. We all agreed that something was not right with the house and sought help from the local priest. We told him exactly what we had experienced and he said he would pop up and bless the house for us. A date was set and he said a prayer in every room and sprinkled holy water. He then said a prayer with us and gave me a holy picture for the house. Since then everything settled. We never found out who or what it was. Maybe it was someone who needed a little help in getting to the other side.

KATHY, DUBLIN

It was in October 1999 that my mother died peacefully in her home. Thankfully she was not alone but surrounded by her loving family at the time of her passing. As I was the last remaining family member to live with her before she passed away, the family home was left to me.

Since my mother's passing I believe that the spirit of my mother is still there. I have never come across more unusual happenings than I have witnessed here. There are times that I can hear footsteps when the house is empty: the sound of slippers gliding over carpet just like my mum's did when she walked around the house and occasionally stepping on a creaky floorboard. There are occasions when I smell her favourite perfume in the air. This is strange as I do not use that brand that she used and it has never been in the home since she passed away.

I have had several unusual experiences in which I felt that Mum visited me in my dreams. I remember in one such occurrence waking up from sleep to see her standing in the doorway of my room. She was wearing the familiar dress and top that I remember she used to wear a lot. I asked her what she was doing here. She told me that she just wanted to see her children again and make sure they were all OK. I remember feeling her touch as she stroked my hair. I remember her walking back out of the bedroom door and disappearing. I turned in my bed and cried myself to sleep. To this day the event seems so real to me. Sometimes I think that I am still grieving but I know in my mind that it is Mum who still visits me from time to time.

I've recounted these experiences to only one other person, my brother, Sean. I was surprised when he didn't call me nuts but rather told me of his similar experience in which Mum visited him in a dream and told him to take care of the young ones. We both had a good cry that day but we know deep in our hearts that a mother's love is everlasting.

THOMAS, COUNTY CORK

In 1986, my brother Mike and his wife Jane moved into a house in Bantry, County Cork. Being newly married they spent the first two years in a flat so this was their first real home. They were like all couples: keen to put their mark on the house, to make it their own home rather than that of the previous owners. Mike and Jane didn't make any radical changes. Rather, they restored covered wooden floors, painted and papered, and filled the home with love. They were very happy there with their two cats but they were anxious to start a family.

From the start, funny things had been happening. Mike or Jane would walk through cold spots. The cats would follow something across the room with their eyes and then run like hell out of there. For some reason I became the object of attention of the spirit. Whatever was in the house did not like me visiting.

The first Christmas my wife and I spent at their house, I was woken up by the sound of the window opening in the guest room and what I thought was someone climbing through it. I jumped up and ran over to the window but when I got there, it was shut. My wife asked what I was doing. I told her what I had just seen. Her answer was 'Get back into bed. You've been drinking too much.' We laughed it off but every time I visited after that it was more of the same: usually a man standing at the foot of my bed or clearly outlined against the window, until I would call out or turn on the lights. Then he would leave. I was never harmed in any way but there were two occasions when he did make contact.

The first time was a hot summer's night. Mike had had one of his barbecue nights and I was staying over. Naturally Mike brought up the tales of my ghostly experiences and the presence in the house. After all the usual laughter at my expense some guests left, some of us went to bed and some stayed up drinking. In the front room my brother James and my cousin Dave were sleeping, one on the couch and the other on two armchairs pulled together to make a bed. Then I heard James let out a cry, 'Got ya!' He jumped up, screaming, 'Get me out of here! I'm going home.' The commotion woke the whole house up. After we calmed James down he explained what had happened. He said he was starting to doze off when he felt as if someone was standing beside him. He opened his eyes to see a figure and, thinking it was one of us messing with him, he lunged out, saying, 'Got ya!' only to see his hand go through whatever was standing there. This freaked him out.

The last time was the night before Mike and Jane were moving to a larger house as Jane was now expecting their first child. We had been up late packing everything, and I mean everything, into boxes for the next day's move. All that remained were the beds we slept on. I was in bed in the spare room. Just before I fell asleep something sat on my feet. I looked down and couldn't see anyone but they were still on my feet. I pulled my feet out from under and saw the indentation of somebody sitting on the bed. I bolted up, grabbed my coat and jeans and spent the night out in my car, refusing to go back into the house until daylight.

ROGER, SLIGO

In 1976, my wife and I separated. It was not an easy parting as we had one daughter. I left the family home and bought a small house in need of renovation not far from my old home. The house took on a new sense of life with a fresh smell to it as the old musty smell went. I redecorated the whole house top to bottom and it was not long before my daughter started to stay over on weekends. Sadly it would all turn pear-shaped. Strange sounds and smells began to come into our lives. The old musty smell returned. Even with my efforts to keep windows and doors open as much as I could, I could not get rid of the smell.

It started with my daughter being woken up at night hearing a rocking chair in the living room. Yet there was no rocking chair in the house. Then my daughter and I kept seeing shadows coming down the staircase as we sat in the living room in the evenings. My daughter's bedroom stayed cold no mater how high I put the heating on. We finally just used this room as storage and I relocated her room to the spare room. From my bedroom I could see across to the door of my daughter's room. I began seeing a shadow every night as regular as clockwork; it would stop outside her door, pause, then look inside but never went in. It was like someone checking on a sleeping child. My daughter was also aware of this as she often asked me if I had checked in on her at night.

Then we began to experience a smell from the downstairs bathroom. It was awful, like the smell of a dead animal. I got a plumber in to check out the drainage system but all was in order. The smell only happened late in the evening just before bedtime. We also experienced bright lights in the garden at night. I was especially worried about my daughter because she has a get-up-and-go type of personality and now all she did was sleep or sit in her room. We didn't even go for walks like we used to. It was so unlike us! Then one night my daughter was up in her room and I was sitting in the living room watching television. I heard her let out a scream. I ran up the stairs. She met me just outside her room in the hall. She said something was in her room. She was reading and happened to look up into the corner. At first she thought it was a fire. A black cloud was forming in the corner. As she watched almost in a daze it seemed to be forming a body shape. When the head began to appear she screamed and ran. She would not go back into the room, not even when I was changing rooms over.

My daughter eventually stopped coming over to visit; she was too afraid just in case whatever it was would make its way into the other bedroom. I sold that house and bought another on the other side of town. I am glad to say that things are normal here and not only do I have my daughter visit but now my grandchildren visit.

GARY, COUNTY GALWAY

I was nineteen years old and in my first year of college in Galway. I stayed with my mum in an old home near the town centre. In the living room there was a wall full of family pictures and a shelf that had more pictures in frames standing on it. One morning, my mum woke up to find all the pictures on the wall were facing the wall.

All of the pictures on the shelf were laying face down. She didn't bother to tell me about this until after I had my own experience.

My mum worked evenings so I was the only one home between 4 pm and midnight. One night at around eight o'clock I was studying in my bedroom. I heard some cupboards opening and closing and water running in the kitchen. I went to say hello to my mum, thinking she had come home from work early. As I walked out of my room I noticed that there were no lights on in the house and there was nobody home but me. I thought I was just hearing things so I left the kitchen light on and went back to my room to study. After about twenty minutes I heard more cupboards banging, water running and pots and pans rattling. This time I was sure my mum was home so I left my room, only to find all the lights in the house turned off again! Turning on the lights, I checked all the rooms and bathroom. After I convinced myself that there was nothing in the house I turned on every single light in the house and returned to study.

After about another twenty minutes, I heard the same sounds from the kitchen as before but I also heard running water in the bathroom, as if somebody was filling the bath. I opened the door and found all the lights in the house turned off again! The taps in the bathroom and kitchen were running on full. I'd had enough. I left the house and went to where my mum worked and waited for her to finish. I told her my story as we walked home. I am not sure if she believed me or not but we never talked about it until my sister came over for a visit one weekend and stayed in my room. As I was away that weekend, I think she just wanted to keep an eye on Mum as she was getting on in life.

My sister was woken in the middle of the night by the feeling of skirts brushing by her arm. Thinking it was Mum she looked up only to glimpse a woman in a white robe pass by the bed and walk through the closed door! She spent the rest of the weekend in Mum's room. As I was due to be away the following weekend also, my sister convinced her husband to stay over with her to keep an eye on Mum. During the night she went down to the kitchen to get a drink of water. After she had poured herself a glass of water, she turned around and was face to face with the 'Lady in White'. The ghost turned around and slowly floated down the hall and into my bedroom where her husband was sleeping.

My sister says she does not know where she got the courage from but she ran into the room and woke her husband from his sleep and recounted what she had just experienced. They both slept in the sitting room on the couch. My sister contacted a psychic medium who then came to the house and carried out what she called a house clearance. Thankfully, whatever it was has left the house and all is quiet now.

ANDREA, COUNTY DOWN
My father passed away in 1991: he had cancer and other health problems. Soon after he died, my sister and I would hear my dad's normal morning routine: the bathroom door closing, then opening, the front door opening then closing, the pots and pans drawer opening and closing. Often we would be woken out of a sound sleep by these noises. Our

mum was the only one never to hear a sound. These noises continued for approximately five years. Then, in 1993, I brought my boyfriend home, knowing that there was no one at home.

After we had spent a while in the house we decided to head down town and get some beers and food. I know I made sure all was locked up before we left the house. When we got home we found all doors and windows open. I thought we had been broken into. My boyfriend rushed into the house but found no one. Nothing had been taken or moved – it was just as we left it, except that all the doors and windows were open. Later on that night, my boyfriend went downstairs to use the bathroom. Just as he turned at the bottom of the stairs he heard a man's voice asking, 'Who are you?' Of course, this sent him running back up the stairs, his heart pounding.

This was not the only experience with that spirit. When I was pregnant with my first son in 1996, there was a presence in the house. It appeared at the top of the stairs, right outside my bedroom door. I was never afraid of this presence; it was comforting, as though it were there to watch over me. My last experience with the spirit was when my youngest son (five years old at the time) told me how much he liked to play with Grandad and that Grandad came to play with him a lot. This broke my heart for I knew in an instant who the spirit was that was watching over me. I got out my photo album and sat my son down and went through the pictures until he pointed out his Grandad, my father. I truly believe he was who he said he was.

COLETTE, DUBLIN

This happened one October night during a Hallowe'en party when I was still in college in 1994. Brian, one of my friends, decided to bring an Ouija board along since it was a Hallowe'en party. He said that he had been using it a lot lately and talking to a spirit he called Joe, who was actually a pretty mean individual.

Brian and a few other people took the board into the kitchen and set it up on the kitchen table with some candles. After about an hour, I went in to see what was going on. There were about ten people there. Brian and a girl named Lisa were using the board and talking to Joe. After a few minutes, another girl, Dana, came in. As soon as she came into the kitchen the glass on the board went absolutely nuts, moving at a frenzied pace. Brian asked Joe what was wrong and the board responded by spelling out, 'I am not Joe'. Then it spelled Dana's name. Brian asked the spirit if it knew Dana and it responded, 'Yes.'

Brian asked the spirit what its name was and it spelt out 'Stephen'. He said he was six years old. Dana went ballistic and started to cry hysterically and ran upstairs. It turns out Dana had a little brother named Stephen who died when he was six. No one at the party knew anything about this; so there's no way anyone could have faked it. After a few minutes Dana came back downstairs and told us that she'd been trying to get in touch with Stephen with Ouija boards over the years but with no luck. So she said she wanted Brian's board.

Well, Joe came back and he and Stephen fought over control of the board. Brian had enough. He put the board in the fire in the living room. This sent Dana off again, crying her eyes out. As you can guess, no one was really in the mood to party after that and everyone ended up either staying at the house the party was in or leaving for home, feeling very weird.

ANGELA, COUNTY DUBLIN

In December 1987 my family and I moved into a house in Swords, County Dublin. We moved in and chose our rooms. Our parents took the largest bedroom and my brothers took the next largest, leaving me with the smallest and the haunted room, although I didn't realise that it was haunted until later on. There was an attic conversion but because it was so cold no one wanted that room to sleep in. The next morning we were all at the table in the kitchen eating breakfast when, all of a sudden, we heard a noise that sounded like someone was walking up and down the staircase leading from the kitchen to the attic. I asked the others if they had heard the noise and they confirmed that they did but dismissed it as a new house – new noises.

Well, strange things started happening from that day on. I heard a massive bang that shook the whole house. I ran outside to see if anyone else had heard that bang or what had made that noise. They all said that they hadn't heard anything. Every night at exactly nine o'clock we could hear a baby crying in the attic conversion. Objects would move from one place to another for no apparent reason. One night I had my CD collection on a shelf in my room. The next morning, they were missing but when I opened my wardrobe to get a pair of jeans I saw all my CDs stacked neatly on a shelf. From time to time bottles of soap would disappear and end up in my closet when

I hadn't put them there. At other times there would be water all over the floor of the kitchen and the taps running even though we always made sure they were off. Another night while I slept on the couch in the living room I was woken from my sleep by the clock radio that went off at exactly 3.10 am, full blast. The clock radio was located in the kitchen on top of the washing machine. I went in to turn it off so it wouldn't wake anyone else up but the clock wasn't even plugged in.

One day my brother and I were out in the garage looking for something when the garage door suddenly shut and I couldn't open it. It felt as if someone was holding the garage door closed by pushing against it from the outside. I tried one last time to open it and was successful. We rushed out just in case it would close again but when I looked back inside, I saw an apparition of a young boy probably about twelve to fourteen years old inside. He was just standing there laughing at us. This scared me so much that I refused ever to go back into the garage.

ANNA, DUBLIN

I first felt a presence shortly after my father committed suicide in our home in Greystones in County Wicklow. I never knew that my dad was suffering from depression. I guess that was something shared only between himself and my mother. I would often smell the scent of his aftershave in the mornings or feel an icy breeze pass by me on the staircase. Sometimes when my mother and I were sitting together in the kitchen having dinner I could feel someone else in the room with us. I would often have friends over who would quickly leave without a reason, only to confess later on that they had seen my father on the stairs. This was the spot where he committed suicide but I had never discussed this with my friends. They even described the clothing he wore on the day he died.

I will never forget the night before my mother passed away. She was lying in bed in our living room. This was necessary, as her illness had confined her to bed. I moved her bedroom downstairs so she could still have friends over. That night she kept looking up the flight of stairs with her eyes very wide and tears streaming down her face. I asked her what was wrong. 'It's your father,' she said. I asked her what she meant. She replied, 'Your father is here for me; it is my time now.' I knew that this was the last night I was going to have my mother alive. My mother smiled at me and then smiled towards the stairs. She was gone. That night my whole world shattered. I was alone and my mother was gone too. Since that night, I hear very heavy and slow footsteps in the house while I am alone. The door to our bedroom (which used to be my parents' bedroom) opens and an icy breeze brushes past me.

Time went on and things changed in my life. I was promoted in work but this meant that I would have to move house and live in Dublin. I had to sell the family home. It was a hard decision but, as they say, life goes on. As I was packing up all my belongings there were constant noisy footsteps during the night. It was as if my parents were unhappy about me leaving. My father even appeared in the sitting room before I finally left. That was one of the strangest days ever. I had difficulty opening the door to my bedroom that morning. It was not stuck but was actually being pushed closed. When I did manage to get it open and get out of my bedroom the door was slammed shut behind me. I could not find the keys to my new house in Dublin. They had been moved from where I had left them and hidden in the press under the stairs. I knew who was doing all this. It got to me so I sat down and burst out crying. All I could say was, 'I have to do this. I need to live my life. Please let me go!' I did make the move to Dublin and I often feel them around me. I do often think about the old house and wonder if the new owners have ever felt the presence of my parents.

PAULA, DUBLIN

In 1999, we moved into our current home, which, we believe, was built in the 1930s. This is a typical Corporation concrete mid-terrace house. After a busy but peaceful first day my daughter and myself were relaxing in the front room when we both heard very heavy and distinct footsteps walk across the floor of my bedroom, that was just overhead. Thinking that there must be an intruder I rushed upstairs but of course there was no one there.

We went to bed that night still feeling nervous about what we heard. I was asleep only a short time when I was disturbed by loud dragging noises across the landing floor. I rushed out of my room but there was nothing there. These noises still occur from time to time and have also been heard by two of my friends. I have also had a coin thrown at me whilst in the kitchen and had the sensation of someone stroking my arm.

Perhaps one of the most frightening and bizarre experiences I have had also occurred when I was in the kitchen. I was preparing a meal for myself when out of the corner of my eye I caught something moving. I turned quickly to see what it was when I saw an empty glass on the counter top move on its own. I was frozen with fear but managed to pull myself together enough to ask out loud if someone was trying to talk to me and was startled by a loud tap on the counter. I asked, 'Who are you?' Then the glass shot off the counter on to the floor and smashed. None of the family stayed in the house that night; my daughters stayed with friends. My husband and I stayed with his mother.

Early next day both my husband and I headed back to the house to get some fresh clothes for all the family, only to find the house partly burned out. There had been a fire in the kitchen and the fire department's report stated that the wiring in the house was the original wiring and had caused the kitchen to go on fire in the middle of the night. He said we were all lucky to have been out that night as we could have suffocated in our sleep from the smoke. Since the fire in the kitchen the whole house has been fully refurbished and there have been no strange incidents anywhere in the house. From time to time my daughter has told me that she saw what she felt was a woman or the shadow of a woman in the house. I don't really know what to make of all this but one thing is clear; on that night someone was watching over my family and used their powers to frighten us out and keep us safe.

COLETTE, COUNTY MEATH

My mother had passed away two years before this incident. My eldest brother Paul had continued to live in the family home, as he was the last member of the family left in there.

All the rest of us had married or moved on. There had been a number of houses burgled in the area and Paul was about to go on holiday. He was afraid that the house would be broken into while he was away so I agreed to house-sit for him. After bringing him to the airport I went straight home to what used to be my family home.

When I arrived at the house I noticed the sweet smell of lilacs as I was unloading the car. I didn't think too much about it at the time because there was always a lilac bush growing there as it was my mother's favourite tree and she adored the scent. Later that evening, as I was watching television I smelled the lilacs again, only this time it got stronger and stronger until it was overpowering. Then as suddenly as it started it was gone. Completely gone. No trace of the smell. I started wondering if something weird was going on.

The next morning I smelled the lilac in my bedroom. I went out to look at the lilac bush but discovered that it had finished flowering long ago and was just full of green leaves. I walked from room to room in the house, smelling everything that could possibly have been the source of the scent. There was nothing in the whole house that could have been the source of the smell. The next day I was again in the sitting room watching television when the lilac smell wafted but this time there was also a coldness in the air as it passed. I had a gut feeling that it was my mother who had just passed me.

From that moment on I could almost feel her around me and in the house at all times. It was not long until Paul returned from his holiday and after the usual holiday chat I sat him down. I asked him out straight had he ever smelt lilac in the house out of season or did anything strange ever happen in the house. His mixed emotions were visible on his face as he looked at me. It was as if he was relieved that someone else had felt it but also sad because he knew it was his mother and because he missed her so badly. He said to me, 'I think it is Mum. I think she is still here in this house. I feel her all the time and I can even smell the lilac in wintertime.' We smelled the scent on and off all summer and a friend of mine smelled it also. I know in my heart that Mum is happy wherever she is and that she is keeping an eye on us in her own special way.

VALERIE, COUNTY WATERFORD
In July of 1997 I was going through a rough and violent separation. My husband at the time had become an alcoholic and was squandering all his wages on drink. The family was falling apart. I could no longer take it so one day I packed up all I could, took my two young children and left him. We went to live with my parents. I decided to fight him through the courts for child support but he was putting up a fight saying I had left him and he wanted me back. I was at my wits' end, almost at breaking point.

It was in the summer. I had my two babies bathed and in bed. I decided to lie on my bed in my bedroom and watch some television. I fell asleep but was awoken by static on the television. The station had gone off the air for the night. For some reason I looked out towards the room where my children were sleeping. I had a habit of keeping all the bedroom doors open at night so that if one of my sons cried, I would hear him.

All of a sudden the bedroom got very cold and I could

see a shadow outside the door of my baby's room. Then a figure appeared: a dark-haired woman in a long red dress. Her hair was tied back but was very long and came all the way down her back. I couldn't make out her face. It was blurry and I just couldn't see it at all. I was in shock. I couldn't move, I just kept saying in my mind, 'My babies, my babies!' I eventually sat up in my bed and just stared at this figure in the doorway of my baby's room. Then she spoke. She said, 'It will be all right. It will be all right.' Then she vanished into thin air. The cold that I felt in my room went as she vanished. I rushed into my children's room to see if they were OK. I found them fast asleep, totally unaware of what had just happened.

Next morning at breakfast my mother asked if everything was OK as she had heard me up and about during the night. At first I decided not to say anything but then I just blurted it out. I told my mother what had happened and described the figure I saw during the night. I described everything; how cold it went and what she looked like. My dad sat there looking at me with tears in his eyes. I asked him if he was OK. He said that he was but he knew who that figure was. I asked him who it could have been and he said it was his mother. He knew it was because of the way I described her, wearing a long red dress, and the colour and the length of her hair. Her hair was dark and very long. He said she was famous around there for the length of her hair. He told me that she always used the expression, 'It will be all right,' to him and his brothers and sisters when they got hurt as young kids. He said he just knew it was his mother. He also said that if she said it would be all right it would be all right.

I eventually went to court to face my ex-husband. I won my case and he had to pay child support. He was ordered to keep away from our children and me until he sought help for his drinking problem. Only after proving that he was no longer an alcoholic and had a stable environment could he seek visiting rights. So it looks like my dad's mum was watching over me and my kids and, as my dad said, if she said it would be all right then it would.

KATE, COUNTY TIPPERARY

After my cousin died in 2000, I had an experience that I remember vividly and which still affects me to this day when I think of it. My cousin, John, died in a senseless car crash while out with friends. He was in the front passenger seat and the crash happened when the driver decided he would drive home after being out drinking for the night. The driver lost control of the car, causing them to crash into a telephone pole on a country road. John fought for his life in hospital but finally the doctors told my aunt and uncle that John had passed away. John was gone and I was heartbroken. I was devastated, as was the whole community, by the fact that such a young life had been so tragically lost and especially as he was his parents' only child.

One night just a few months after his death, while I was asleep in bed, I had some sort of dream that was different from any other dream I ever had before or since. This was what I 'dreamt'. I was walking in a park when I looked over towards some trees. I don't know why. I just felt drawn to them for some reason. I saw my cousin John. He was just standing next to a tree. I said, 'John, what are you doing here? I thought you died!' He said, 'I did. I'm just making sure everyone is OK.' Then I remember saying, 'Can I come over to you?' He replied, 'Yes.' So I walked over to him and said, 'I'm so sorry for everything, John. I'm so sorry for the crash.' His reply was, 'It was not your fault; you weren't even there. I'm fine; don't worry about me.' Then he hugged me and I can still remember vividly being pressed against him, holding him close: he was so cold to hold. I know it was not a dream because when John left I just lay there in my bed crying till it was morning time.

At first I didn't want to tell anyone but finally I told my mother. I somewhat expected her to get angry or mad as she was fond of John also. All she said was, 'That's interesting.' She asked me if she could tell my story to John's mother, her sister. I said that I didn't mind, but that I hoped it would not upset her. It was a few days later when my mum met up with John's mum. Then my mum called me at home and asked me what John was wearing in the dream. 'A white shirt with a blue pattern, jeans and desert boots,' I said. 'Why?' There was a pause on the phone but in the background I could hear my aunt crying. Then my mum said, 'Well, apparently that's what he was wearing when he died.' I hadn't seen John on the night he died or ever known what he was wearing that night, yet in what was or was not a dream I saw him in the clothing he was wearing when the car crashed. John never visited me again. I'm hoping that some day, when it's my turn to go, John will be able to meet me and I'll be able to see him again. Something tells me he'll be there.

DAVID, DUBLIN

When I was about eighteen my grandmother died. She had been very ill for a number of weeks but was actually doing better. I was at college and just hanging out in the grounds of the college when I saw her standing at the top of a path that led to the main entrance. Standing beside her was a man I did not recognise. I thought this very strange because I knew she was in hospital. I started to walk towards her when she spoke to me. She said, 'No, you cannot come with me. You must stay here.' I froze to the spot. Next thing I knew my classmate was shaking me saying it was time to return to class. This I did but kept looking back towards where I had seen my grandmother standing. I was in class for about forty-five minutes when I was called to my principal's office. He asked me to sit down. 'David,' he said. 'I have some very bad news for you. There is no other way to say this but your grandmother has passed away. I am so sorry.' I will never forget those words.

It was during the wake that I discussed what I had seen in college with other members of the family. One of my uncles asked me to describe the man I had seen with my grandmother. He said it was my grandfather I had seen. I never knew my grandfather as he died long before I was born. I asked my mother if she had a picture of Grandad for me to look at and there he was. The man I saw at my college was in the photo. Grandmother and Grandad were together again.

Later on that day my brother and I were discussing my grandmother's death and he told me that I was not the only one who had seen her. He was in a different school when she died and could have sworn he saw her in the hall. He had also been told by one of our cousins that he had seen her at his workplace and that his brother (my other cousin) also thought he had seen her outside his home on the day of her death. Our conclusion was that our grandmother had always been an incredible source of strength for all the family and people around her and that she could not leave this world without saying goodbye to the people she loved. We truly believe that she came to visit each of her grandchildren on the day of her death.

EDWARD, COUNTY LIMERICK

In the early 1980s, we lived in a house in south Dublin where a previous tenant had died in her sleep and a man who practised satanic rituals had lived. We didn't learn these things until we had lived there a couple of years. By this time, evidence had mounted that we were not alone in that house.

My first experience was being woken in the middle of the night by someone or something touching me on the shoulder. I turned to see who it was but there was nobody there. My partner and I joked about it for some time, saying that it was the spirit of the old woman who died in her sleep a few years before.

The second incident was a couple of months later. It involved the sheets of the bed being pulled down hard on each side. Now this time it affected my partner as she felt the sheets being pulled. I was unable to sit up against the force. As the pressure released I heard a faint giggle. This freaked us out. We jumped out of bed, grabbed a blanket and slept downstairs in the sitting room.

Some time after that we took in a lodger to help pay the mortgage. He stayed in the back bedroom, which was always cold and creepy. I recall he had a difficult time sleeping in that room on a number of occasions. With the extra money from the new tenant we were able to replace the carpet in our bedroom, which had been laid by a previous tenant. When we lifted the old carpet we found symbols of the occult painted on the wooden floor. Some of these symbols would have been directly under our bed. We sanded the symbols away and laid the new carpet.

Shortly after that we began to hear noises, like someone walking around downstairs. Then these noises began in the bedrooms. At first we thought it was the lodger moving around at night. But one night we heard steps coming up the stairs. They stopped outside our room but then came inside. This was scary, as the door did not open but we both heard the footsteps in the room. These happenings escalated so much that the tenant could no longer stand it and he finally left. A female tenant quickly replaced him. She experienced the same 'touch' on the shoulder as I did. Her description of the feeling was the same, even though I had never told her of any incident related to the house.

I then had to change jobs and with the new job came night shifts. To make my partner feel somewhat safer, I bought a dog to keep her company at night. At different times it would run to the kitchen and bark at nothing. It would look directly at something we could not see and growl. I could never explain that. Late at night, you could hear the cupboard doors opening and the drawers opening and closing. My girlfriend always thought it was the old woman wandering around the house.

Through work I got the contact details of a medium and asked him if he could help us. He agreed and came over to the house. He said it was an active house with several spirits. Some were attached to the property but some came in uninvited. He asked us if we ever played with the Ouija board or the occult. We had never done so and told him that. We also told him about the markings we found when we were changing the carpet. He performed some kind of cleansing, as he called it, in all the rooms, and one for us. He said that it was a troubled house and that it might need several attempts to clear it.

That night we went to bed with hope that things would get better. But we were wrong. We were woken that night by the sound of what I thought were burglars in the kitchen. Our dog that was in the bedroom was going mad, snapping at the bedroom door and wanting to get out. I jumped up and let him out and he darted straight for the kitchen. I followed and when we got to the kitchen it was trashed. All the contents of the presses were emptied on to the floor. All the drawers were also emptied; the whole place was a mess. What scared us the most was that there was nobody there and no sign of a break-in. The whole house was locked up as we had left it before going to bed. We could take no more. We had lost two tenants and now it was terrorising us. We moved out and sold the property.

I often pass that way out of curiosity. The house is still there. I don't know who lives there now but I always wonder if they experienced the same things we did.

THE KELLY FAMILY, DUBLIN

This strange experience happened while we were on a family holiday in Killarney, County Kerry. We stayed in an old castle that had been converted into a hotel. The room was a family suite; it had two bedrooms and a sitting room. The first night we stayed there I thought I saw something move out of the corner of my eye but quickly dismissed it as my overactive imagination. Then strange things started to happen: objects going missing and turning up with no explanation and strange noises in the room at night as if someone was in the room with us. There was also a horrible feeling of being watched by an unseen being. I felt that many times and to tell you the truth, I was scared to death more than once! One strange incident occurred just a couple of nights into our stay. At first I thought I was going crazy, until my husband experienced it too.

We arrived back at the hotel after being out for the morning. We went up to the room to freshen up before heading out later for the evening. Now kids will be kids and they love to race ahead of us into the room. As we got to the room the door was open and our children were in their bedroom. As I entered the room I saw a man sitting on the bed in our bedroom. I grabbed my husband to show him and he saw him also. He approached the man saying, 'Excuse me but I think you are in the wrong room.' The man looked at my husband and vanished. Well, we all left the room. We gave our children some money to go to the bar for some soft drinks and we asked to see the manager. The manager politely asked us if there was something wrong. We explained what we had both just witnessed in our room. What shocked us both was that he did not seem surprised. It was as if he had heard it before. He asked us to describe what we had seen in detail to him.

I said that when we entered the room I had seen him first and then pointed him out to my husband. The man was in dark clothing sitting on the edge of the bed with his head slumped forward. When my husband said to him, 'I think you are in the wrong room,' he just vanished. The manager went on to explain that the hotel was reputed to be haunted by one of its former owners. He has been seen around the hotel and in our room on several occasions. We were given a new room for the remainder of the stay and the manager apologised to us for what had happened. We were more concerned about the children than about ourselves.

We never saw or felt anything else for the remainder of our stay in the hotel. I have no doubt in my mind that the hotel is haunted and, strangely enough, both my husband and I wish to return without the children and stay in the same room now that we are over the initial shock.

JAMES, LIMERICK

The house I grew up in was haunted. No matter what room you were in you never felt alone. We lived in a two-bedroom townhouse in Limerick City. The front door opened into the living room and straight back was the kitchen. On the right-hand side was the staircase that led to the bedrooms. My parents' room was on the left side in the hallway across from the bathroom. This may help you to picture better where things happened.

Every night I would make sure the doors of my wardrobe were closed and almost every night the right side would open. Some nights the noise would wake me and I could see a man standing at my wardrobe. He looked like something from an old black-and-white movie and I couldn't distinguish any features. He never moved or said anything. He would just stand there. At first I was so scared that I would jump under the covers, terrified to look. Now I am used to seeing him. I had two windows in my room. One looked out at the backyard; the other at the neighbours' house. They had no windows on this side of their house. Sometimes at night I could hear someone walking the length of our house in the backyard and if there was a moonlit night I could see a shadow pass across the window even one floor up.

One night I woke up to the feeling of someone staring at me and I looked towards my door. My mum was standing there looking at me and she just turned around and walked down the hall. I thought this was really weird; so I got up to see what was wrong. I looked down the hall and asked, 'Mum?' and whatever it was turned around and disappeared, at the same time smiling at me.

Another night I thought I was having a nightmare. In my nightmare, I was lying on my side facing the wall and I heard a deep male voice say, 'Don't turn around or I'll scare you to death.' Needless to say I did not turn around, as it was not my father's voice. He does not even have a deep voice. I felt fingers go around my throat but I was too scared to scream or move. Luckily they didn't tighten their grip but slowly released. I felt them slide along my neck. Next thing I knew was my mum coming in to wake me up for school. I started to cry and told her about my nightmare. She could clearly see finger-marks on my neck and woke my dad up. They searched the whole house and all the doors and windows were still locked from the inside. No one but us was there. My mum concluded that I had scratched myself in my sleep but I did not believe her.

The garage at the back had an attic above it that could only be reached through a small hole in the ceiling. There were no stairs to it so my dad always had to use a ladder. Sometimes my parents would ask me to babysit my younger brother while they went out. They would make sure I locked the doors to the house before they left and my dad would have already locked all the bay doors so no one could get in. Almost every time they went out and left us alone I would hear very clear, very loud footsteps walk across the bedroom floor toward the stairs. My dad usually left a few lights turned down low so he and my mother could see when they got back in but they were bright enough to see everything in the house. The footsteps always came from my bedroom and stopped at the stairs at the landing just outside my parents' bedroom. No one ever came down the stairs. I never saw anyone walking up them either. I only ever heard the footsteps.

At other times I could hear a woman's voice calling my name in the middle of the night from somewhere inside my room. If my friends stayed the night they could hear it too. One night my best friend and I were home alone and we heard what I could only describe as a woman screaming out loud. We ran outside on the back porch and as soon as we shut the door behind us we couldn't hear it any more but if we opened it we could hear it again. We later found out that long before we lived there a man had hanged himself from the attic door that was just outside my bedroom and that his wife became a recluse in the house until she was also found dead. But she died of natural causes; she did not kill herself.

MICHELLE, COUNTY WICKLOW

My mother passed away from complications resulting from chemotherapy in March 1989. Two years later, in September 1991, I lost my father to a heart attack. I came from a traditional family with old beliefs and respected the dying wishes of both my parents. So there was a traditional wake for my father in the family home. He was laid out in my parents' room and friends, family and relatives packed the house to pay their last respects. I recall wandering from room to room making sure that everyone had enough tea and food. Then at 10.30 am – I remember looking at the clock – I suddenly caught a glimpse of someone going into the room where my father lay. I went in just to see who it was but there was nobody there. I just brushed it off.

I then recall being drawn to a woman standing in the hallway of the house, her face turned slightly away from me. She was standing just inside the front room when I got closer to her. I immediately noticed her clothing. She was wearing a blue flowered blouse and a dark-blue shawl. I thought for a second, 'She's dressed exactly the way my mum used to dress!' Then she turned her head towards me. It *was* my mother! I cannot emphasise this enough; it was her. I *was* looking at *her*. I had not laid eyes on my mother for two years since she had died but she looked as real as any other person in the room. My mother did not say a word but smiled sweetly at me and slowly started to fade away to nothing. My eyes filled up until tears started running down my face. I knew then who it was that I saw go into my dad's room where he was laid out. I felt as if I was not there, yet I was.

I was brought back to reality somewhat by my sister shaking me saying, 'Are you OK?'

I looked at her with tearful eyes and said, 'Yes, I'm OK.' I told her we had just had a special visitor.

'Who?' she asked, looking around the room to see whom I was speaking about.

'It was Mum; she popped in on Dad.'

My sister give me a look of, 'You shouldn't be saying things like that,' until she looked into my eyes. Then her eyes filled up for she knew I was not lying. Dad's funeral was the next day but I don't ever remember being sad that day, because I knew where he was and who he was with. I would like to think that when my time comes to pass over to the other side someone will come to collect me.

TRACY, COUNTY DUBLIN

I lived in Ashbourne, County Meath, in 1982. One night my father was driving the family home from the town along a country road. My father was driving with my mother in the front with him and in the back were myself and my two brothers. The car broke down and we had to pull over to the side of the road. I recall my mother giving out as she was always at Dad to get a better car as this one was always giving trouble. My dad tried to start the car over and over again but it just would not start.

Suddenly we became aware of someone coming towards the car. We could make out that it was a man and he was walking up to the driver's side of the car. As he got closer we noticed he was not walking a normal walk; it was more like a march. His clothes were also strange. He was wearing a uniform which was torn and dirty. As he got into full view we could see that his uniform was not only in a mess but it was all bloody. The man continued to march up in front of the car, crossed over and disappeared into the ditch. We were all terrified. My dad got out his torch and searched the ditch but the man was nowhere to be seen.

We couldn't believe what we had seen but we all knew that we had indeed seen it. My dad eventually got the car started and we were all thankful to get away from that place. We were curious to know who or what we had seen. My dad went to a local historical society and told them what we had seen. He described the man and what he was wearing. We found out that during the 1916 Rising rebel soldiers were killed in this area by the British who occupied Ireland then. We are now convinced that on that night we saw the ghost of an Irish rebel walking along that road. To this day my mother will not let my dad drive her along that road at night. I am now grown up and have my own car, but unlike my mum, when I drive down that road, I always hope to see the figure again.

ORLA, COUNTY CLARE
We bought an old house in County Clare that was built in 1877. It was in a dreadful state and took three months just to get one room ready to live in and the kitchen and bathroom habitable. We moved in and spent another six months getting the rest of the house together. When everything was finished and we had furnished the place, we settled back to enjoy the fruits of our labour. It was only

after this that we started to experience some odd things happening.

While we were renovating there was a cat that never left the house so we took it in as a pet. We don't know where she came from but she was a wonderful creature. One night I was woken up. My side of the bed was surrounded by freezing air. I lay there, unable to do anything but then I reached out for the cat who slept on the bed and the freezing air started to warm up and my terror subsided. Then on other occasions we would be sitting in front of the television and suddenly the cat's head would turn and stare intently at one place in the room. It would stand up, back arched, its fur standing up on its back. I had a wind chime hanging in the kitchen and sometimes it would sway violently as if someone was brushing very hard against it.

A friend came to visit one evening. At one point he went up to the bathroom, then came rushing down, grabbed his girlfriend by the arm and rushed out. He said he had seen a ghost on the landing upstairs and he wasn't staying another minute. Another night we were sitting in front of the television with a cup of coffee each on the coffee table and something/somebody knocked very hard on the table twice. I don't know if this was a previous owner of the house.

Then one night I was looking out the kitchen window. I was just gazing out into the empty darkness when all of a sudden I felt a tap on my head like someone playing tricks on me. I looked at my reflection in the window against the darkness but there was nobody beside me. I called out to my husband but he was in another room. He came into the kitchen and I told him what had just happened. It was at that point that we started to put everything together and realise that, in fact, we were not alone in the house. Another evening I was in the kitchen again, but this time I was washing dishes. I saw a tall old man, dressed in black, walk through the wall next to the presses. This caused me to drop a glass I was washing. It smashed on the floor. I looked at the broken glass and then back up to where the old man had been but he was gone.

After that, I saw him quite a few times, walking in and out where there is now a wall but where there was once a back door to the house that we bricked up to make the kitchen bigger. Then I started to see an old lady who looked like something out of the Victorian era. She appeared only at the top of the stairs and nowhere else in the house. There is a corner in the front room that is permanently freezing cold, even if we have the central heating and a fire on – it doesn't matter how warm the room is, that bit stays cold. We considered moving out and either renting or selling the house but my husband would not entertain either. We did, however, get the house blessed and this worked for a while but things are slowly starting to happen again.

KAREN, DUBLIN

I lived in a flat on the north side of Dublin five years ago with my then husband. The place was a council flat. I hated it from the moment I went in the door. The first morning we were there my husband went to work, leaving me in bed. I woke to hear the sound of what I thought were boxes being shuffled around the floor. (We had left all our boxes in the front room waiting to be unpacked.) I got up and as I went to the door of the front room the noise stopped.

From then on there were countless incidents: doors that I knew had been open were suddenly shut; things moved around; the cupboard where I kept my saucepans flew open and the saucepans were thrown around the room one night; the heating was turned up full while we were asleep; the lights were turned on when we were out; and taps turned full-on. Also everything electrical seemed to be affected: a kettle blew up when it was not even switched on. When we tried to play music there was always a horrible humming noise coming from the speakers and we had a total of four television sets that broke while we were living there. Before breaking down they would all make a crackling sound. As it was a council flat we could not just move out so we were stuck there.

Then my husband started a job as a security guard, which meant working some nights. I had my two little dogs that I had left with my mum come and live with me for company. They would suddenly start barking and would seem to be attacking nothing. I mean *I* could see nothing. I got used to all the odd things after a while and just thought that as nothing had hurt me so far I would just put up with it. One night while my husband was at work I was woken from my sleep by the sensation of someone sitting on the end of my bed. I jumped up and switched the bedside lamp on and looked around the room but could see nothing. My two dogs were barking like mad outside my bedroom door. When I opened the door to see what was wrong with them they darted into my bedroom and started to bark at my bed.

Two nights later my husband went out to buy some cigarettes and I was left alone with the two dogs. I was watching television and sitting facing the kitchen door which was shut but which had glass panels. Suddenly the dogs started growling and ran towards the closed kitchen door but then they both backed away, still growling. I sat and watched the shape of a man walk towards the door. It stood still for maybe a couple of seconds then walked through the door and into the sitting room. It continued to walk until it went through the wall of the flat. I knew what I'd seen but just did not want to believe it. My husband returned from the shops to find me a nervous wreck. I sat there bawling my eyes out as I told him what I had just seen. He said I must have fallen asleep and had a bad dream or something.

That night while we were in bed the dogs started growling and barking again. They were in the front room. After my evening's experience there was no way I was getting up so I made my husband go. He went out into the front room to see what was up with the dogs. He came flying back, absolutely terrified, and described seeing the 'apparition' exactly the same way as I had seen it. That was that. We left the flat that night, never to return. I was always sure that there was an evil presence in the flat. All these years later what I experienced in that flat is as fresh in my mind as it was when it happened.

ELIZABETH, COUNTY WATERFORD
This occurrence actually took place outside Ireland, in Stafford, UK, in May 2002. I had gone to visit my sister and nephews in England. While I was there, I slept in my nephew's room as he was away from home with the army.

The second evening that I was there, we were all sitting

in the living room watching a movie. I heard a noise down the hall and looked up to see the door to the bedroom that I was staying in (my nephew's door) suddenly open. I looked around but no one had moved from their seats. I said, 'Did anyone else see that? That bedroom door just opened by itself.'

They all looked at one another and smiled. A few moments later something fell off the shelf in that bedroom. I looked around and said, 'Now, I know you all heard that.' My sister went into the room and found her son's alarm clock on the floor. It had been on that shelf for months. There was no reason that it should suddenly have fallen. After a few minutes, my sister told me that they felt they had a ghost in the house but that it had never bothered anyone, just things.

Once she heard music playing in the middle of the night and when she came out, the stereo was on but nobody else was up at that hour of the night. Pans and dishes would disappear from the kitchen, then reappear weeks later. The sliding glass door would open by itself. At this point, I was feeling freaked out.

I went to bed that night doubting that I would sleep but, after a while, I did fall asleep. I woke up to the sound of a tapping on the window. The tapping seemed to move from the window to the walls and go around the room. I got up and flicked on the light. The tapping suddenly stopped. I sat there with the light on for a while, then decided that it must have been my imagination or maybe the wind outside and I turned the light back off. As soon as I did, the tapping started again. There was a cold clammy feeling in the room.

I jumped back up and turned the light back on and again the tapping stopped. I got up and went to get my sister. Together we looked outside to see if anything could have been hitting the window. There were no bushes, trees or wind to have caused the tapping that I heard. She checked out the room and there was nothing there that could have been causing it. Not knowing what else to do and feeling embarrassed that I had awakened my sister, I told her that I was all right and to go back to bed. Once again I turned off the light to try to sleep and the tapping started again.

Then as suddenly as it had began, the tapping stopped. There was an eerie silence in the room and I looked over to see a white figure move towards the door and disappear through it. Needless to say, I didn't sleep too much after that. I was glad that I was only staying for a long weekend and I could not wait for it to end. When I returned back home to Waterford I told my family about my creepy weekend and they just laughed. I know what happened did happen and that I was not going crazy.

SUZANNE, DERRY

Twenty-five years we moved into a house ago that had an interesting past to it, one that we didn't find out about until later.

As it turned out, one of the previous owners had been diagnosed with bipolar depression and had lost his will to live, so he killed himself by hanging himself from the rafters in the garage. Now whether or not that has to do with the house or not remains to be seen but there have been many unusual happenings that leave us to ponder who or what is responsible.

We have seen shadows move across the wall, movement out of the corner of our eyes, someone knocking on the front door when there is no one there and other unusual events. However, there are two prominent occurrences that hold solid memory for me due to their strangeness.

The first one was the sound of someone constantly bouncing a ball in the attic over the bedrooms. It was noisy, yet it had a pattern and rhythm to it. It would go on for a few minutes and then stop for a few minutes. However, it always seemed to build up when we were in the bedrooms and it never moved to any other part of the house.

I encouraged my husband to get up into the attic to see if he could find anything that could be making the noise. He went up into the attic but could find nothing loose, not even a ball that could make the noise. My husband is not psychic or anything like that but when he got down from the attic he said that he felt as if someone or something was watching him. As he was placing the attic door back in place we both heard someone call my name. Now, it wasn't clear like a normal person talking; it was like listening to a radio station that wasn't quite tuned in.

We dismissed it and didn't think too much of it until later that night when we were in bed. I heard the voice again at the door to our room. I sat up and felt that someone was in the room. I woke my husband from his sleep and told him what I had heard. He got up and checked the whole house but there was nothing out of the ordinary. Some time later I was telling my brother about the strange happenings when he announced that he had an Ouija board and asked if I would like him to bring it around and try and find out who it was. I agreed. I thought it would be fun for a nice night in and to see what we could find.

We did it a little differently, with only one person at a time using the planchette while being blindfolded and with the board always turned a different way so we couldn't 'cheat'. After asking the name of the spirit that was in my house, I received the answer, Owen. This happened three times to myself and my brother. We each had different feelings in our hands when we were holding the planchette, ranging from cold to hot and from the feeling of being held to being pushed. It was very interesting, although some may call us foolish for using the board: we wanted to see if there was anything paranormal in the house. Nothing much happened that night apart from the feeling of hot and cold, and the name Owen being spelled out on the board.

I dropped my brother and his wife home and I drove back into my driveway and up to the garage that I had left open knowing I would only be a few minutes away. It was then that I saw him. By that I mean the previous owner. I saw him hanging in the garage just as when he committed suicide all those years ago. I stopped the car dead and hit the horn to alert my husband in the house. He came running out to see what was wrong. I pointed to the garage but he saw nothing. We got the house blessed by the local parish priest and we all said a Mass in the garage for the spirit of the previous owner, Owen. Since the blessing there really hasn't been much activity in the house. I'm not sure if it went away or if it's dormant for now, waiting to be woken up again. One thing is for sure: the Ouija board will never again be allowed into the house.

ANNE, COUNTY LOUTH

I was about thirteen or fourteen years old when this happened to me. It was quite a few years ago, as I am twenty-seven now, but I remember it as if it was yesterday.

I was home alone. My dad was at work and my mum and brother had gone to the store. I was reading a book on the couch in the family room. I had my back to the kitchen and all the rest of the rooms in the house. All of a sudden I heard heavy footsteps, like a big man's boots, walking really fast through the kitchen. I turned around quickly but there was no one there. It really scared me. I checked around the house and did not find anything. So, I sat back down on the couch, this time facing the kitchen, and tried to get back to reading my book. Needless to say I was very happy when my mum and brother came home from the store. I have heard some other things in the house at night. My brother has also heard them. Sometimes late at night around two or three in the morning, we heard what sounded like a bunch of people running on the roof. It was pretty loud.

My mum and dad have heard the noise too. We really don't know what it is. We were never really scared by the noise; it happened quite often. One night when we had some friends staying over and stayed up really late talking, the noises came. Our friends were freaked. We told them the noise always occurred late at night.

My parents have seen shadows on the walls in the hallway when the bathroom light is on. They have seen shadows going into different rooms throughout the house. They have also felt 'watched' while lying in bed. My parents told me that they have heard footsteps too. I only heard them once and that was enough for me. My parents said the house was empty when we moved in. I don't know what kind of history the house has had or when it was built.

MIKE, COUNTY DOWN

My story is quite lengthy, as I have had a lot of things happening to me and my family. So bear with me.

My story started when I was about ten years old. My dad and the rest of our family built a new house in County Down. We had lived there for about three months when it first happened. My sister and I had our own rooms. When we went to sleep we would always close the bedroom doors, to find them open in the morning for no apparent reason, or we would leave one open just to see what would happen and the next morning find that the open one was closed and the other one was open.

My sister was about five years old at the time and every morning she would come running into my room and jump into bed with me and say that the wardrobe door was sliding open. When everyone was in bed I would hear the drawer in the kitchen open and slam shut and the next morning we would go to get breakfast and find a knife on the counter with the blade pointed at the wall. When we walked down the hallway the light would go out. When we were in the middle of the hall it would come on when we least expected it. My dad checked the wiring and he never found anything wrong. We felt as if we were being watched all the time and this freaked me out.

My second experience happened when my grandmother died of cancer in hospital. My grandmother lived in Dublin but the night she died I saw her sitting on my bed and she told me that everything was going to be OK and that she would never leave me. She also said that when I got married and had kids she would be there as well. Then she kissed me goodbye and vanished. After she left I had an overwhelming sadness and I knew that she was dead. Three hours later we got a call from our family in Dublin saying that she died at the exact time she came to me to say her last goodbye.

My next experience is the kind that happens every day now. My wife and two boys (twelve and nine) and I moved into a 1930s farmhouse. We had been there for about three days when my kids started to freak out when we walked out of the bathroom and left the door open. We could never figure out why, until I went to take a bath and left the door open because I was alone in the house and felt there was no need to lock it. That is when it first happened to me.

The door started slowly to close and I just sat there and watched it finally shut all the way. Needless to say my bath was cut really short. Well, I got used to this and even thank whatever is doing it from time to time. The only time I am scared is when I feel as if someone is watching me in the bathroom. Then I ask it to give me privacy and the feeling goes away.

My wife works nights sometimes as she is a nurse in the local hospital and as I sit in the living room I get the most horrifying feeling and don't want to look at the kitchen. I can't stop myself, however, and I catch a glimpse of a small woman-like shadow. Then it's gone, and I feel better. Sometimes I feel as if someone is tucking me in under the bedclothes and looking in on my boys. The smell confirms it. I get a whiff of my grandmother's perfume and I just say, 'Thanks Grandma!' I tell her I love her and I sleep peacefully that night. I can live with the spirits here; they make me feel safe.

ALISON, DUBLIN

We moved into our house six years ago. After a few weeks I was woken up by the sound of people talking downstairs. It sounded like females talking loudly. The next morning I asked my mum what she was doing downstairs at five in the morning. She replied that she was nowhere near downstairs during the night. This went on for weeks: voices waking me up at all hours of the morning. One night I woke my sister Suzanne up and thankfully she could also hear them. After that the noises escalated, from talking, to banging, to moving furniture around the kitchen. I was always too scared to go down to have a look. Ghostly footsteps and doors opening on their own quickly followed but then things started to change.

The noises were not confined to downstairs: I could hear them in the bedroom as well. We could also hear children playing in the house at night. While all this was going on, one of my sisters, Marie, was complaining of a pain in her stomach. This was happening every night. The noises then escalated to the point where all family members could hear them and one night we thought the neighbours were having a party but in fact the noise was coming from our house. On another night we heard banging on the ceiling above us. We knew that there was no one upstairs so my mum hit the ceiling with the handle of a brush and to our amazement we got a reply in the form of more banging.

Then the spirits switched their attention to all the

electrical appliances within the house. The washing machine would knock itself on and off. The electric fan over the cooker would come on by itself. Lights would be switched on and off by some force but it was when a lava lamp that was not even plugged in came on that things really started to freak me out. Not that I was not freaked out enough. In my bedroom my radio would change stations on its own. I went to see a local medium to see if he could pick anything up. It was an OK reading and when he was finished he asked me if I was OK with it. I answered no and said that I had come there for a reason. His answer freaked me out. He said, 'I know and she is standing beside you.' He told me it was the spirit of a friend of mine who had hanged herself four years earlier. He also told me that she said she was sorry for messing with my radio and also that she was glad that I had kept her clothes. (You see, we always swapped clothes). My father, on another night, saw a black shadow move right around him while he was alone in the room. Then, while my dad and I were in my bedroom, a table in the room moved across the floor.

At this point we decided to seek the help of another medium to see if they could give us any answers to these ghostly happenings. When she visited our home she informed us that it was an extremely active house and that there were not one or two but several spirits present. First off she explained to us that at the end of Marie's bed there was the spirit of a little boy named Michael, who was playing tricks on Marie at night. Her recommendation to cure Marie of her stomach pain was to put salt and purified water under her bed. This we did and Marie's stomach pain ceased straight away.

When the medium was in the kitchen that night she told us that there was a spirit of a young girl looking in the window and that it was associated with the mother of the family, who unknown to her had had two miscarriages. She explained that she was a very quiet spirit that was happy to be with her family. She also revealed that in my mum's room there was a spirit of a young boy, also by the name of Michael: he was not a harmful spirit, but there more to protect her.

The medium also picked up on a poltergeist that was roaming the house. This would tie in with the fact that my father and other males in the house were being assaulted. This would range from being pushed to one receiving a black eye, whereas all the females in the house felt a gentle touching of the hair when they were in bed. Then to our amazement, when she entered the sitting room on her room-to-room psychic search of the house, she pointed to the corner of the room under the staircase and our worst fear came true. She explained to us that there was a vortex and that there were, in fact, lots of spirits wandering in and out of our home. She picked up a spirit of a man with a walking stick in the sitting room, a spirit again called Michael, a poltergeist in my room and the spirit in my mum's room. She also felt that area of the room to be extremely cold.

The medium explained to us that there was a spirit in the room trying to make contact with someone in the family. She asked us if anyone had died belonging to us. My mum answered no but then thought about my friend and asked her to ask if it was Niamh Byrne. She got a definite yes as an answer. Niamh was my friend who hanged herself.

The medium told me that Niamh was jealous of me and disliked all the boyfriends I had in the house. When she left she said that there was very little she could do for us. We still live in the house and the strange ghostly happenings continue to keep us awake and somewhat amused.

MARY, LONGFORD
When I was twelve years old my parents moved into a house that had been empty for a couple of years. From the first day we moved into the house I knew that there was something odd about it. It was little things at first. There was the feeling that I wasn't 'wanted' in the house. Within a few months I became afraid of the stairs and the dark and being alone, especially upstairs. I tried to tell my parents but they did not take me seriously and even teased me about my fears at times.

I didn't start seeing 'him' until after I was thirteen years of age. He was always just at the corner of my eye. I would turn my head and he would be gone. He was always at the bottom of the stairs during the day. At night I could feel him coming up the stairs. I knew if I told my family they wouldn't believe me and would tease me even more. I saw him quite regularly until I moved out of the house when I was eighteen years of age. All that time I didn't tell anyone about him. I was more afraid of people thinking I was crazy than I was of actually seeing him.

Years passed and I convinced myself that it had all been in my imagination. I married and eventually had a daughter. She would spend some nights at my parents' house on a sleep-over as she loved them so much and they loved her even more. I never at any time mentioned the ghost to her. Two years ago my daughter and I were watching a Hallowe'en special on TV and we started to talk about ghosts. That is when she asked who was at the bottom of my parents' stairs. I nearly fell off my chair! She would see a cloud at the bottom of the stairs and at night she would see it coming up the stairs. I told her that it was just her imagination and that I had never seen anything in my parents' house while I lived there but deep in my heart I knew she had seen the ghost of the man I had seen as a child.

DAVE, COUNTY TIPPERARY

My wife Laura and our four children Thomas, Noel, Kim, and Robert, lived in a house located in Ballynahinch, County Down. It was very old, a big spacious two-storey house. The rooms had tall ceilings and a large Victorian feel to them. The floors did have a small slant but I was used to that. Everyone was happy living there except Laura. She said she got a weird 'vibe' from it when she was alone in the house. This, coming from a woman who has heightened sensitivity to the supernatural, like seeing ghosts and people's auras from time to time, did concern me just a little bit. Out of the blue Laura asked me if I could pick up an Ouija board while I was out so we could play with it that night.

An Ouija board is supposed to let you contact the dead. I used to play with one years ago as a kid but stopped when it became a little scary. One night Laura took out the Ouija board and both of us began to play with it. We began by asking it various questions and getting short uninformative responses, until we asked the person for a name. Laura looked at me, startled, and asked, 'Did you hear that?' I said, 'No.' She then said she heard a small girl's voice say 'Sara'. I rolled my eyes without her seeing me. I hadn't heard it and thought she was hearing things, like maybe a kid outside yelling at someone else.

A few days later, my two youngest boys, who were four years old at the time, got up for breakfast. As they ate, they chatted about a girl they had played with in their room the night before. They told us her name was Sara. Laura jumped in and asked them several questions but didn't get much out of them, just that Sara was in their room playing with toys but she never spoke a word to them. It was then that Laura told me that she had actually seen Sara but was afraid to tell me because it might scare me. She told me about Sara and the other two ghosts she had seen since the Ouija board. 'Two *other* ghosts? Oh great,' I thought to myself. As we lay in bed that night, Laura told me that Sara's sharp, clear image was that of a little blonde girl with long hair probably four years old. She said that Sara would sometimes stand at the entrance to our bedroom and look in but would never enter.

This really freaked me out. Laura then went on to describe the other two ghosts. The first of these was a man, maybe in his late thirties. He was dressed in a brown suit that appeared to be from the 18th century and he wore two-tone shoes. He had dark hair that was unkempt. He had clear features but was more transparent than Sara. Laura said that she would see him sometimes standing at the top of the stairs looking down and that she saw him once in the bathroom. He didn't move much, just stood around. Laura said she tried to talk to him once but he just disappeared. The second of these ghosts appeared to be a woman from the same era as that of the man, with her hair piled high and with a long puffed-out dress. Her image also travelled up and down the stairs but very slowly. The image was very faint with no detail at all, just an outline.

Over the next few weeks, I would occasionally ask Laura for any ghost updates and she would tell me if she had seen them or not. We kept the appearances secret from the kids, not wanting to scare them. The two younger boys had not mentioned Sara either since the first time. A week later, Laura and I were chatting in bed when all a sudden Laura started staring at the door. I asked what she was staring at. She said that flashes of light were shooting over the bed, one at a time. Then she told me Sara was at the door again. Well, I can tell you my heart was pounding in my chest so hard I could hear it. I said to Laura, 'Tell me if she comes in.' Just then, Laura said she was in the room. I looked around the room but didn't see or feel anything. I looked at Laura and said 'Where is she now? I cannot see her.'

'Sara is standing right by the wardrobe.' I didn't see anything and didn't feel anything. I started feeling stupid. Was this a joke Laura was pulling on me? So far, everyone except me was seeing things. I stared transfixed at the wardrobe but saw nothing. I then shouted out, 'This is a load of codswallop.' I felt so silly at seeing nothing that I had to say something. I must have fallen asleep at some stage.

The next morning when I woke up, I went to give Laura a good morning kiss when she shouted out, 'Jesus! You'd better go to the bathroom and look in the mirror.' I got up and went upstairs to look. I started to shake just a little when I saw a long scratch across my cheek. 'You shouldn't have yelled at Sara,' Laura said.

A few days later, my eldest son Robert came running downstairs from his bedroom, screaming. He said a man with a brown suit was standing in his room, watching him sleep. He described the same man as Laura had and at this point I started to believe the house was haunted. Robert would never make anything up like this. Besides, he knew nothing about the Ouija board or what Laura was seeing around the house. I decided that it might just be time to move house. At night, I started hearing footsteps upstairs when no one was there and sometimes the stairs would squeak like someone was walking on them. Screw this! We finally moved into an apartment about ten miles away from the house. No ghosts followed. My boys still remember Sara. I made Laura burn the Ouija board but she has kept up her abilities to hear and see spirits and one day she hopes to become a medium to help others.

BARBARA, COUNTY WICKLOW

When our son David, who was five years old, came into our bedroom at around three o'clock one morning he said he was upset and that he'd had a bad dream. As usual we allowed him to climb into the bed between us. I asked him to tell me about his dream, as I believe that when you tell your bad dreams to someone they leave the conscious mind and don't appear again. He told me that he saw a little boy in his room. I thought this was all in his imagination so I asked David, 'Where is the little boy now?' David's reply shocked me. 'He's sitting in your wardrobe.'

Our wardrobe door was open and I could see very

vaguely the white clothes hanging. It was too dark to see clearly, he said. I thought, right, David's imagination was working overtime. So I asked, 'What's his name?' I was thinking that David wouldn't be able to think of a name quickly enough. He said, 'Sean.' This sent chills up my arms because I realised that he was telling the truth and that he really had seen the little boy. My immediate reaction was 'Stop, David! You're scaring Mummy.'

The next morning, while David was at school, I was in the kitchen wiping down the counter, thinking of nothing much except what to prepare for supper. All a sudden the name Sean Connolly came to me. It was freakish, like when you say something at the same time as someone else. Sean Connolly was my nephew who was very sick when he was born. Sadly he died when he was just two years old. I was very close to him as he was my only brother's son.

My brother and his wife are very religious so I was not able to tell them abut this as I felt that they might think I was crazy. I could hardly believe it myself. When David came home that afternoon he went upstairs to his playroom. It was some time later that I heard him talking to someone. I shouted up to him, 'Who are you talking to?' His answer sent a shiver down my spine. 'I am playing with Sean.' I didn't want to go upstairs in case I scared him away. I then asked David a kind of test question as I was still trying to hold on to what sanity I had left. I asked, 'What does Sean look like?' David described Sean exactly as he had been during his life. I must add that we had never had a picture of Sean in our home so David could not have known what Sean looked like.

I believe that it was the spirit of my nephew, Sean

Connolly, who visited my son. We have since moved away from the town of Brittas, County Wicklow. Since we moved, my son David has never spoken about Sean again. I often wonder if the new owners of our old home have ever experienced Sean or was it just David who was blessed with Sean's visits.

MICHELLE, COUNTY CORK

I can't really explain what this incident could be. Maybe it was our imagination or maybe just some weird coincidence. But it did happen. I live in Cobh, County Cork. I was at the time babysitting my friend's child for some extra spending money. It was a small family that had recently had a new baby. Also that year, unfortunately, they had a death in the family. A grandfather who had lived with them for quite a while had passed away a few months before. He had taken care of the newborn whenever the parents were not around.

My friends have this intercom system placed in the baby's room. Whenever the baby moved or cried you could hear her through a walkie-talkie sort of thing that came with the intercom system. Sometimes the frequency got mixed up and you could hear music coming from it. Sometimes it was the local radio stations but that was only if you had the walkie-talkie thing tuned into the wrong channel.

On this particular night I had a female friend from college stay over with me as I was babysitting. My friend and I were watching television in the living room and the baby was fast asleep in her room that was at the back of the house. The intercom system was placed on a table right next to her crib and the walkie-talkie was placed on a coffee table in the living room within hearing range. We could hear her soft even breathing letting us know that she was sound asleep. A while later we heard the baby making gurgling noises. We didn't make much fuss over it. A little bit later we started to hear her making more noise as if she was waking up and was getting ready for her famous tantrum crying.

My friend started to get up to go and quiet her down but I said not to as she might quiet down on her own, 'Just give her some time.' So my friend sat back down and the noises eventually stopped. About fifteen minutes later we heard noises again. This time the baby was awake and beginning to cry softly. My friend got up to go into the baby's room to settle her but before she got to the room we could hear on the walkie-talkie an old man's voice telling the baby to hush and be a good little girl and not to make so much noise. We looked at each other and darted into the baby's room, thinking we had an intruder, but we found the baby safe in her crib and all windows were shut. We both know what we heard and we both knew it was not our imagination playing tricks on us. The baby quietened down and we returned to the sitting room but some time later we could hear the old man's voice again quieting her down and talking softly as if putting her back to sleep. We could also hear soft patting on her back, as you would usually do when you wanted to quieten a small baby. Again we dashed into the room but as before we could find nothing and all the windows and doors were secure.

Later that evening when my friends returned home from their night out, I could not help it; I had to tell them what I had heard on the baby monitor. I told them that there was no one else in the room, yet both of us had heard it. I instinctively knew by looking into my friend's eyes that he too had heard it and when I looked at his wife I could see tears standing in them. At that point all he said was, 'I'll explain it to you tomorrow.' The next day he rang me, true to his word. He explained that they believed that the voice of the old man that we heard on the walkie-talkie was the spirit of his wife's grandfather returning to take care of the baby.

It was very long ago but I still remember the incident as it sort of frightened me. Afterwards I continued to go over to my friend's house and nothing else out of the ordinary happened.

STACY, COUNTY DONEGAL

When I was seventeen I moved to Dublin to start my first career as a receptionist for a city-centre hotel. It was an old mansion converted into a hotel. I was fortunate to get one of the flats just down the road. At first I heard only from guests about their experiences: things like people wanting to move rooms from the main building to the newer areas of the hotel. Some said they heard children crying or felt an oppressive atmosphere in the rooms. At first I took this as overactive imaginations as a result of reading a guide to the hotel that said the old hall was reputed to be haunted. There was reportedly a bloodstain on a ceiling that would not go even when painted over. This turned out to be a leaky rusty pipe.

I worked there for a couple of months with no problems; then slowly things got a bit strange. The first thing happened when I was in the back office at reception. I was on shift with three other girls and I glanced up at the security camera and saw a figure walk up to the desk and go round the back of the office as if to come to where we were. I thought this was a thief, so immediately ran out to catch him. There was not a person in sight. Thinking it was just my imagination, I gave no more attention to it. I worked the next evening shift on my own but I couldn't shake the feeling of being watched for the whole eight hours. The atmosphere seemed kind of electric but in the way that you can hear a static kind of sound, which affected my ears as if I was on a plane. Whenever other people came it seemed to lift, but would then return. I went home to my flat, which is a two-minute walk across the car park, but I had a weird feeling, as if I was being followed, so I ran all the way.

From this on, inside my flat didn't feel the same as before. My flatmate, a girl called June from Mayo, also noticed the atmosphere but only when I was there. She was into the paranormal; so I thought it was wishful thinking on her part until one night in particular. I had been at work and things had started to happen, things like feeling someone brushing by me when I was on my own and objects moving. This didn't scare me at the time but I started to believe there was maybe some truth in the ghost stories. I collected a myriad stories from other workers who all claimed beyond the shadow of a doubt that the place was haunted by more than one ghost. The hotel had been a stately residence before being converted into a hotel. I started a ghost tour for the American tourists, which broke up my day and gave me a chance to gather more stories and get extra tips.

Then it started to get quite scary. One night my flatmate had gone back home so I was in bed with my partner. I couldn't sleep so I lay facing the edge of the bed. Next thing I saw what I thought was John, my partner, walk across the room and stand beside the bed. I was just about to ask him what he was doing when I felt movement. It was my partner still by my side. I panicked, knowing it was not John or a burglar, and screamed. I didn't see it disappear because I turned over to wake John up.

When June returned I told her about my experience. She said that she had never seen anything in the flat before but that I walked in an aura followed me. She said that as we talked she followed its movement with her eyes all the time and it never left the room. She said that she would invite a friend of hers who was a medium over to see what he thought of the place.

A couple of nights later the medium arrived over. After the usual greetings and light chat he put his hand out and said there was a lot of energy in this place. He assured me it was nothing malicious, which eased my mind.

A few nights later I slept in my room on my own, which was a rare occurrence: after the vision of the body standing beside me my partner stayed over as much as he could. I went to sleep, not giving a thought to our guest, but woke up with a feeling of absolute terror. I lay there scanning the room but couldn't see anything. I called for my flatmate but she slept soundly. The feeling wouldn't go away, so I ran into June's room screaming. She looked completely shocked. I am not a timid person; so she knew something had happened by my reaction. Once I left the room, though, the fear went away. In a sleepy haze I went back to the room, proclaiming to June that everything was all right now. I went back to bed and slept soundly but she couldn't sleep and ended up sharing my bed for the night.

The more fearful I got, the more the whole thing escalated. I was woken a second time when I was asleep alone but this time there were several odd things around the light bulb (which was off). The only way to describe them was like the crystal balls David Bowie spins in *Labyrinth*. I again ran into June's room and I started sleeping there whenever my partner didn't stay.

Things then started to happen more often at work, especially when I was on my own. I think now, looking back, they were playful tricks more than anything else but they terrified me. A key would fall from the cubbyhole where keys were stored. I'd put it back and then another would fall at the other end. Pens would go missing and turn up again. I would feel someone put their hands on my hips or push past me but no one would be around. I finally decided I had had enough of living in fear and I hated the job anyway. After a year of living there I left the flat and the job. Whatever happened in that hotel in its past life has left some sort of scar that time does not seem to want to heal.

VALERIE, COUNTY DUBLIN

I moved to Dublin from Sligo in 1997. I moved into a flat just beside Christ Church Cathedral. One night after drinking alone, I decided to play with a Ouija board. I had purchased it about a week earlier, just for kicks. That night I lit several candles in the living room and started using the board. I had no results after approximately fifteen minutes so I decided to go to bed. The next morning, however, I was awakened by my bull mastiff, Zoose, who was locked in the bedroom with me due to the fact that he was a vicious dog and had to be kept muzzled and away from strangers.

This particular morning I was very tired and was facing the wall near the bed when Zoose began barking loudly. I figured he wanted to go outside so I told him to shut up. When he continued to bark I turned my head in his direction and saw him barking at the bedroom door as if someone were behind it. Then I saw the door slowly open about four inches before Zoose jumped up on his hind legs, closing it. Scared, I got a baseball bat which I kept under the bed and stood near the bedroom door. I shouted out that I had a dog and a bat and I was going to let the dog loose. I listened intently, expecting to hear footsteps running about the flat but did not hear anything. After building up enough courage I let Zoose out of the room. The dog just ran in circles around the living room barking as if he was really upset while looking all over the room.

As I left the bedroom, I noticed a very strong smell of perfume in front of the doorway. I can only describe the perfume as something an old woman would wear. It had a flowery, sickening smell and would not dissipate. After checking all the window and door locks of the apartment, I went back to the bedroom and found that the flowery smell was still outside the doorway. I could walk through it and it would not go away. It just stayed there in the same spot for almost thirty minutes. About a week later the same thing happened. Zoose would continue to bark at my bedroom door as if something was on the other side.

Since the previous time I had developed a habit of

leaving the light on in the hallway just outside my bedroom overnight. As Zoose was barking at the door I could see the shadows made by someone walking past my door in the light shining under the door. I was full sure someone was in my flat. I jumped up and grabbed the bat and let Zoose out. As before he ran into the front room and continued to bark at nothing that I could see. The flat was empty except for myself and Zoose. I then began to remember the night that I played with the Ouija board. I began to wonder if I had indeed brought something over from the other side.

It was then that I contacted a very good friend who knew more about this sort of thing that I did. I explained everything that had happened and he suspected that I might have brought something into my flat. He suggested that he pop over and asked if he could bring a friend who was a psychic along. I agreed – as if I was going to refuse any help! A few nights later they arrived and it was not long before the psychic friend began to pick up on the spirit of an old lady. I asked him was it because of me playing with the Ouija board. His reply confused me a little. He said, 'Indirectly, yes. Do you know a woman by the name of Brigid?' I was shocked. Brigid was my grandmother, who had passed away when I was young. So I replied, 'Yes I do.'

'Well, she does not like what you are doing with the Ouija board and she is here to ask you to stop.' He said that she did not come through the use of the board but she had always been keeping an eye on me. She was here to warn me to stop messing in what I did not know about before I got hurt. He went on to perform a cleansing of the flat using incense. We lit a fire as per his directions and we burned the Ouija board. Since that night I have never been woken by Zoose barking and that also tells me that my grandmother Brigid is not in the flat. I do sometimes feel as if she is with me but this could be in my imagination but at least I do know that she is keeping an eye on me from afar. I am surprised that the manufacturers of the Ouija board have not been forced to stop making these items. I will never go near one again as long as I live.

TREVOR, DUBLIN

I am originally from England but now live here in Dublin. This ghostly manifestation took place when I was at my boarding school in the south of England. I was sleeping in a dormitory with about eight or nine other boys when I was awoken by a bright but soft light shining down on me. I opened my eyes and saw a figure standing over my bed. Its face was clear; it was a boy one or two years older than me. He had stopped at the foot of my bed and a soft radiance was coming from his face. The face and the figure of the apparition were transparent and he was wearing a long gown. It was definitely looking at me as though it was trying to communicate with me. I was not at all afraid. None of the other boys in the room woke up.

I sat up in bed so I could see the dormitory clearly around me. By this time the figure had turned and floated across the dormitory and faded through the door at the other end of the room. The figure was about two feet off the ground and appeared to have no feet. The entire manifestation probably took only about ten to fifteen seconds. I lay back down in my bed and fell fast asleep. Next morning when I woke up I just thought it had all been a bad dream. Later that day after study I discussed my dream with the other boys from the dorm. It was then that I began to realise that it was in fact not a dream but something that I had experienced as other boys from the dorm had also experienced the same manifestation.

I later found out that a boy had collapsed and died at the school after running a race on the summer sports day five years previous to this. The boy had apparently suffered a medical condition and had died at the school as a result of the severe physical strain of the race. The doctor and nurse had tried to revive him in the sick bay but to no avail. He died five years before I saw his ghost. I searched through the school photograph records and I recognised the face of the ghost due to its resemblance to the picture of the young boy who died tragically.

I also found out that another boy had heard singing in the school chapel in the early hours of the morning when everyone was asleep on the same night I had seen the apparition. The boy who had died had been a choirboy at the school. Around about the time I saw the ghost, another boy saw the ghost in the school library for a few moments during the day. I have no doubt as to the identity of the spirit but it wasn't a haunting, rather a visitation as it only happened a few times and never happened again, at least during my remaining three years at the school. I remember all the details about what I saw as if it were yesterday; it was in fact, some twenty-five years ago.

SARAH, COUNTY DOWN

I am an experienced Ouija-board user but when I first started to use it, I didn't know the 'rules'. For example, never use the Ouija board alone. Unknown to myself I broke the second rule and I did not realise the consequences. Myself and my friends, Clare and Lorraine, moved into an apartment together. There were three bedrooms. One day I was telling them about the fun Ouija-board experiences I had and they refused to believe me. So I invited them to join in one evening just for the fun of it. They decided to give it a try that night. I told everyone to meditate, to pray or focus their own minds to be clear. We then took turns in pairs using the Ouija board because I knew that spirits sometimes were fickle about whom they were communicating with. For example, I seldom get a response directly on the Ouija board and it's usually my friends that have to operate the board. However, I'm the one who's usually asking questions to make sure that no one is fooling around on it and making up answers.

We were asking silly questions about some lost items and funny stuff and we eventually received some communication. We asked leading questions to find out just what it was that we were in communication with. It replied and we thought it was the spirit of a young boy. It gave its age as ten years old and said it had blonde hair. Eventually it asked if it could come and play with us. I said, 'Yes,' at the time, not knowing I had given it power into the physical world. When we were finished playing with the board and talking to the spirit child we packed up the board and put it back under my bed where I kept it. A couple of nights later, when I was in the shower, I heard Clare, my flatmate, screaming. I ran out dripping wet and asked her what was wrong. She was crying and hysterical and telling me that she saw a pair of eyes staring at her from the wardrobe and demonic laughing coming from there. When I looked I didn't see anything, nor did I sense anything – except for my adrenalin from hearing her scream!

Later that night when Lorraine came home we discussed what had happened to Clare. We all agreed that it had something to do with the Ouija board. When they asked me to get rid of it from the flat, I agreed. I went into my bedroom to throw away the Ouija board, knowing that it was the cause of the problem. When I went to reach under my bed to retrieve the board, all a sudden I felt as if I had put my hand into a deep freeze – like the feeling you get in the supermarket when you reach in to get something from the frozen section. Nothing was there physically but my arm was all tingly. I didn't sense any presence besides the physical sensations so I quickly grabbed the board out from underneath my bed and darted back into the sitting room. I tore up the board with my hands.

After a while we all calmed down and went to sleep. I could see that Clare was still a bit shaken by what had happened and I did not like the sensation that I felt under my bed so I asked Clare if she would like it if I slept in her room with her that night. She was delighted with this so we settled in her bed and watched some television until we fell asleep. All of a sudden I felt Clare sit up in bed. She pointed at the wardrobe door which was closed and said out loud, 'Go away!' Then she put her head down and went right back to sleep. Curious I woke her and asked her if she remembered her dream. She looked sleepily at me and mumbled that a little kid had been running in and out of the door saying, 'I'm gonna get you,' every time he ran in and out. I told her that the bedroom door had been closed the whole night. At this she seemed confused and she said that it was open and that while I was watching television a child had kept coming in and out. I asked her to describe the child, thinking maybe it was the same spirit from the board. She described the boy from the board. This of course freaked me out even more.

A few nights later we had a party at the apartment to try and liven up what had now become a very dull serious feeling in the apartment. I told a few of my friends about what had happened. It seemed that one of them had had a similar experience. I asked him how he got rid of the unwanted spirit, as we felt that it was still here. He said that he had to burn his board as it was the only way of getting rid of any unwanted spirits. I looked at him in horror. 'What's wrong now?' he asked. 'I only tore it up and put it in the bin. I did not burn it.' Then I remembered that the rubbish had not been collected yet. So there we were digging through our rubbish in the early hours of the morning. God only knows what the neighbours were thinking. We managed to get all the pieces. We lit a fire with old newspapers and magazines in the apartment. Then we burned the Ouija board. I am serious when I say this but you could feel the oppressive atmosphere leaving the apartment as we watched the Ouija board burn. After that night nothing else strange happened and we all agreed never to bring another Ouija board into the apartment. I joined a psychic development group and have learned how to use an Ouija board correctly now and would not advise anyone to use one without being trained. There is a lot I did not know about them that I do now.

NORMA, COUNTY GALWAY

We moved into our current house nine years ago. Shortly after we moved in, I started feeling a presence in my bedroom – most often when I was alone in the house or after everyone was in bed. Our television started going on and off by itself. We'd come home from work and the radio or television would be on. I didn't feel any threat from the presence, but I was very aware of it and a little scared. My husband always had some practical reason for what was going on – so, for instance, we gave the 'broken' television away. Each day when I came home from work, I'd put my jewellery in my jewellery box. Certain pieces of jewellery (earrings and one particular necklace) would be missing, then turn up later – after weeks or months. Once my husband found a necklace I thought I'd lost two years prior lying on a dining room chair.

Two or three years after living here, I began to see the shadowy outline of a tall woman in a long black dress. I saw her repeatedly over the next seven or eight years, always in my bedroom. One day, I was sitting on the bed and drops of water kept falling on my arm. I automatically looked up at the ceiling. The tank in the attic was above our bedroom but it was not leaking. I realised it was the woman and that she was crying. I told her that I knew she was there and that she was sad and that I hoped she would just leave our house and go to heaven so she could be in peace. We're Catholic and I have crucifixes in almost every room and a few Bibles around. I went to church that day and said a prayer for her, that she might find everlasting peace. That's the last time she was here – there has been no sign of her since.

Last year, my thirteen-year-old daughter and I were watching a haunted film on television and she told me that she'd seen a real ghost before. I asked her about it and she said she'd seen 'a tall woman in a black dress' in the hallway of our house. She said she could sometimes feel the woman standing over her bed stroking her hair. I don't know the history of the house. I only know that I never really believed in ghosts. Now I know that they exist and are absolutely real and capable of expressing love and sadness, just like living people. I only hope she's found peace. I'm pretty glad that we're not being watched all the time. It is a little scary. The weird thing is that my husband never saw her and still thinks I'm crazy!

ALEX, COUNTY CORK

I have lived in Cork all my life. Like many girls growing up I longed to be a nurse. Sadly life dealt me a bad deck. I had a hard upbringing and did not get the right grades in my exams to make it as a nurse. This however did not deter me from my lifelong wish. I studied enough to make it as a nurse's aid and got a job in a nursing home.

Not long after I started working there I heard other employees talking about the ghost of a little girl but I dismissed the idea. It seems as if every nursing home and hospital has that type of haunting circulating about it. I worked the 3 pm–11 pm shift and one of my jobs was to put the residents to bed. Most of the residents had severe cases of Alzheimer's disease. Most were able to talk and carry on a conversation but if you had a conversation with them, left them and approached them five minutes later, they had no idea who you were, let alone remember that they had just had a conversation with you. It is important to remember this because it proves that what I am about to tell you is not my imagination, nor it is not a case of the residents trying to pull a fast one on the employees.

I remember the first time I heard one of the residents talking about the little girl. It was a resident talking to himself in his room. I went in to see what was going on. I asked him whom he was talking to and he said, 'That little girl right there.' Of course, I did not see anybody. Another time, a woman was having a hard time getting to sleep. I asked her what the problem was. 'That little girl keeps coming in and talking to me,' she said. This type of thing happened to me often – usually at least two or three times a week. It occurred with several different residents, not just two or three, and they all described the little girl in exactly the same way. She was about five or six years old, wore a bib and a long dress and had long, black, curly hair. She never caused any harm and there was no physical evidence such as things moving on their own. It was always the residents who were in a confused state of mind who saw her. Residents who had all their mental capacities never saw her; nor did employees.

I did some research and found out from some local people who have lived in the area for years that about fifty years ago, before the building became a nursing home, it was a private residence and a little girl was killed there. Apparently, she fell down the staircase and injured her head. She was unconscious when she was removed from the house to hospital but never regained consciousness and died a short time later. Her parents were so upset by this that they could not remain there, so they sold the house. If it was not for the fact that most of the residents who saw her suffered from Alzheimer's I would have put all this down to an old wives' tale but I cannot. I still work at the nursing home and residents still report seeing her. I now accept her as part of the building and as long as I never see her I will remain there. Hearing about her is one thing but I don't ever want to see her.

CATHERINE, COUNTY WEXFORD

Twelve years ago my husband and I inherited my mother's home in County Clare, after she died from cancer. She lived alone in her home as my father had died some years before. This house is at least sixty years old and ever since we moved into it some weird things have been happening.

The first hint of anything weird was the constant switching on and off of lights at the top of the stairs, which slowly spread to switching on and off of the light at the bottom of the stairs. I witnessed this happening myself and so did another friend. Things would disappear and turn up in places that had been checked several times before! Then one night Patrick, my husband, was drinking a glass of beer. He put it down next to him, and I saw him doing it, but when he reached down to get it again it was at the opposite side of the room!

About three months after this he bought a dog to keep him company. Things have become much worse since the dog has entered the home. The dog barks at points on the walls, which he follows with his eyes. Another time I was taking a bath and I placed a towel on the sink beside the bath. Patrick was in the dining room. When I was finished having my bath I went to get the towel to dry myself but it was gone. I shouted at Patrick to stop messing and give me back the towel but he said that he had not taken the towel. I could hear him coming out of the dining room and up the stairs. It was then that he said that the towel was on the stairs but I know that I placed it on the sink in the bathroom.

The worst things occurred over a three-night period. It was during the winter so we had been sleeping with a big blanket over the top of our bed. Well, on the first night. I woke up to find the big heavy blanket had been rolled up and placed across the bottom of our bed. I woke Patrick to show him. I have to say this is the first time I have ever seen my husband really freaked out.

The next night we went to sleep as normal and when we woke up the next morning we found the doors of the wardrobe open and all the clothes from our wardrobe scattered around the bedroom floor. Also the chair from in front of the computer desk that had been in the corner of the bedroom had been moved and placed against the door, as if to try to stop somebody coming in!

The third night was the worst. I woke up with the sensation of being pinned down in the bed. It was as if someone very heavy was lying on top of me. I found it hard to breathe. I tried to turn and wake Patrick but all I could move was my head and I could see Patrick sound asleep. I could not even shout out for help! I must have blanked out at that point. I remember waking up the next morning and the bedroom was as we had left it. Nothing had moved. Patrick was still sleeping. I lay there thinking about the night and what a wild dream I had just had but the reality of the night sank in when I went to take a shower and found bruises on my legs and my upper arms. I screamed the house down and Patrick came running into the bathroom to see what was going on. I was so hysterical that it took me a while to fill Patrick in on what I had experienced during the night.

At that point we could take no more. I moved into Patrick's parents' home while Patrick cleared our personal belongings out of that house. We sold off all the furniture and put the house on the market.

We now live in a nice semi-detached here in Wexford. I am glad to say since that hateful night nothing else has happened. I do not know if things continued to happen in my mother's house or not and to be honest I don't care either. I don't know what all this means or why it happened to us. It has changed my life and I believe that there are forces working in our lives over which we have no control.

VAL, COUNTY OFFALY

When my husband and I married six years ago, we bought our first home from a family member who was selling it because she had gone to live in a nursing home. We had been living at Nora's house for about a year and a half when we received word that she had died during the night in the nursing home.

The events I am about to describe began a week after Nora's death. I started with my husband, Tom. Several times while he was out gardening in the back – Tom loved his gardening– a woman called his name. He returned to the house each time and asked me why I called him but I hadn't called him. Then the radio in our kitchen malfunctioned; it would change stations without any of us touching it. We finally unplugged it and packed it away.

After we had disposed of the radio, the television began to act up. First it would turn itself off. We assumed it was overheating. But it started changing channels by itself just like the radio – just random channels – and would then turn itself off. After a few weeks of this, the television started coming on by itself in the middle of the night and we'd have to get out of bed and turn it off. Sometimes it would come back on as soon as we had got back into bed. We took it to a repair shop three different times and it always functioned just fine. But when we returned home it would malfunction again.

One day, while we were sitting at the kitchen table talking and having coffee, a dark but transparent 'form' came from the dining room, walked behind my husband and disappeared. My expression must have been one of sheer terror because my husband immediately asked me what was wrong. The form resembled a shadow of a woman. It had a female shape but no features. This happened to me again and twice to my husband. We would trade places at the table in the hope that we would see it. We are both convinced that it was the spirit of Nora.

One night at about 1.30 am I got up to go to the bathroom. I thought I heard Tom down in the kitchen but when I came out of the bathroom he was still in bed. I woke Tom, telling him I thought there was someone down in the kitchen. Tom and I went down together to the kitchen. This time we saw the form but it was like a glowing white mist. It came straight towards us but we slammed the door shut and ran back up the stairs. We were terrified by what we had seen.

Another instance involved a coffee cup that our son had given my husband for Father's Day. It was one of those 'Best Dad in the World' cups. It was badly chipped but my husband didn't want to discard it for sentimental reasons, so we stored it behind some dishes on the top shelf of an old china cabinet in the dining room. One morning when I got up and went to the kitchen to make coffee, that cup was sitting in the sink! I checked the china cabinet but the other dishes were undisturbed and unmoved. My husband and son swear they didn't take it out.

We have since moved to a new home. I must admit that with the exception of the night in the kitchen we never felt threatened by this presence, although it was scary. My husband and I have often talked about how when one of us would be alone in the house, we never really felt 'alone'. The day we moved, I stood in the middle of the house and invited 'Nora' to come with us. When I later told my husband what I had done, he laughed and told me he had also invited her to join us. She didn't come, however. We love our new home but it certainly lacks the feeling of presence the old home had.

DANIELLE, COUNTY CLARE

I grew up in a fairly rural part of Ennis, County Clare. When we were in school, my sister and I used to babysit for a family a few streets over from us. Their house was adorable. It was a two-storey building with a steeply pointed roof. The family had two girls that my sister and I went to babysit. On summer nights, they sometimes had another little girl friend over to stay with them.

After giving us the obligatory last-minute instructions,

and 'in case of' advice, the parents headed out for the evening. They hadn't been gone an hour when a thunderstorm came up, shortly after we'd fed the children dinner. The thunder started off with low rumbles, gradually building up in intensity over the next fifteen minutes or so. The children, being children, got scared during the storm, hanging on to my arms and legs and screaming shrilly with each crash of thunder. I could see they were getting more and more frantic so in an effort to distract them, I dragged them into the living room where I seated them all on the couch and put on a film for them to watch. With a promise to get goodies from the kitchen for them all if they would be quiet and watch the movie, I got a blanket and tucked them in where they sat in a row on the couch. I went to put the film on.

When I stood up and looked back across the room, I could see through the living-room door into the dining room. As I looked, the roller blinds on the dining room window rolled down closed. Seriously, they closed by themselves. Not wanting to attract the attention of the children to what I had just seen, I stepped quickly out into the hall and yelled for my sister. She answered from upstairs, where she was changing the baby's nappy. I looked back into the living room and the blinds were still shut. There was the strangest feeling that something was there watching me. My sister came downstairs with the baby and went into the kitchen, talking and cooing to the baby as she went. She eventually came into the living room with us and I whispered what had happened to her. She gave me one of those looks that said, 'What planet are you on?' but when she saw the expression on my own face, she seemed convinced. She looked into the dining room and back at me and then at the children.

My sister and I sat on the couch, pretending that nothing was wrong. It was then that we heard a noise from upstairs. The children, thankfully, didn't seem to be paying attention to it but we looked at each other and got up slowly, heading out in the hall and following the sound to the foot of steps. I took the baby and we went up a couple of the steps. 'What is it?' I asked but my sister just shook her head. We listened in silence on the stairs till we realised what it was. The tap in the upstairs bathroom was on. My sister, thinking that it had been left on by accident somehow (we were grasping at straws), went upstairs and turned it off, as she had been the last one up there. She came down and we turned to head down the hall but no sooner were we back in the living room than we heard it come on again. This of course freaked us out. It happened several more times that evening even though we kept turning it off.

Unlike a normal night, we did not put the kids to bed but kept them with us on the couch. They all fell asleep and my sister and I watched television until the adults got home. We didn't mention it to them but when we got home I told my mum about it. We decided not to babysit in that house again but agreed to mind the children at our place instead.

COLETTE, COUNTY OFFALY

My mum, my sister and I were visiting my uncle in Dublin. His house was too small to accommodate us all so we stayed in a B&B just a short distance from his place. The B&B was one of those huge Dublin flats in a house that was divided in two. The ground floor and basement belonged to the old couple. They were the owners, and the first and top floor made up the B&B where we stayed.

The first night my mum went out with my uncle and we watched television in the room. We suddenly heard this loud noise, 'Boom, boom, boom!' above us and our first reaction was: 'Gee, the other guests above us are noisy.' But when it happened a second time I said to my sister, 'Hang on; there aren't any guests above us; we are on the top floor.' As it was windy we went to see if there was a branch banging the roof but there was nothing. As we were going back up the stairs to our room I said to her, 'What if it was a poltergeist?' She just gave me a silly look.

Next afternoon I came into my room from shopping, dumped my bags on my bed and went back out. I stopped short as I closed the door. Something wasn't right. I went back in to find all the paintings and mirrors on the wall slightly tilted. That night before we went to bed we straightened all the pictures and the mirror on the wall. When I turned out the light I heard a scraping noise. I turned on the lights just in time to see the mirror on the wall right in front of me had tilted to one side. I asked my sister if she had seen it also but she had not. She *did* notice that the mirror she had straightened was now tilted.

The next night my sister and I returned to the B&B early. We started to watch an old movie on the television in the sitting room when the 'Boom, boom, boom' started upstairs above us. We went to investigate but when we got upstairs the 'Boom, boom, boom' started downstairs. We had now told my mother all about 'the ghost' but she dismissed it as our overactive imaginations and our not being used to the noises that this house made. We went out that night and she went to my uncle's. On her way back in the taxi she said, 'I hope that my kids are back as they say the house is haunted.' The taxi man said: 'Don't worry about ghosts. They can't hurt you if you just tell them politely to go away and if that fails recite the psalm that begins, "The Lord is my shepherd…"'

My mother got into bed, turned out the lights and said to herself; 'How nice! The cat's come to sleep on the end of the bed with me,' before she realised that there was no cat in the house. We came in at that moment to hear a very squeaky little voice saying, 'Please go away, please!' and then beginning to recite, 'The Lord is my Shepherd…' That night it got worse: doors slamming, 'Boom, boom, boom', cold gusts of wind, the works!

Thank God that was also our last night at the B&B. Two months later our uncle contacted us asking us if we had experienced anything while staying there, as there was a report that it was haunted. Another guest had experienced some strange things but he went to the papers with his story. The report in the paper also had a comment from the owners of the B&B who said, 'It's the spirit of the owner who first lived there. His spirit is still there but he's absolutely harmless.' I often wonder who it was in the B&B making all those noises and if indeed it was the spirit of the previous owner, but one thing is sure: I will never stay there again.

PAUL, COUNTY DONEGAL
This happened around 1992. I had split from my girlfriend whom I had lived with for two years so I needed a place

to stay. The company I worked for rented property so I approached my boss to see if I could rent one of the units. He was OK with it as business was business. I moved in and everything was fine. After a while I met a very nice woman called June (whom I eventually married) and things were looking up for me.

One weekend I decided to stay with her but when I returned home to my place it was as if someone had burgled the place. Stuff was tossed about; they left it in a mess. But as I began to tidy up, things did not seem right. The front door that I used to come in was secure and none of the windows were open or looked like they had been tampered with. It was Christmas time and among the mess, I found all the Christmas presents for my family and my girlfriend still wrapped. This was strange. I figured that some kids had got in and had some fun but left when disturbed. But how did they get in? I was baffled.

The next night I woke up in the middle of the night. I heard footsteps walking around the room next to mine. I thought they were back to finish off the job. I jumped up and got my baseball bat from under my bed. I listened to the footsteps get closer to the door of my bedroom. They stopped right outside my bedroom door. I lunged out, expecting to catch whoever it was in my place, but it was totally empty. I searched the entire place but there was nobody. So I figured I was dreaming it and went back to bed. I could not sleep a wink. I kept running the whole incident through my head.

My new girlfriend and I were hanging out at my place on St Stephen's Day. I had not told her about anything that happened. I did not want her to think I had lost it.

We were watching a film on the television but after a while I fell asleep. Suddenly she woke me up. 'Paul, Paul!' she whispered urgently. 'There's somebody in here! Listen!' I woke up and heard the same heavy footsteps outside the door, going back and forth. Then the noise of a chair from my kitchen followed. Screeeech! It was as if the chair was being pulled across the floor. I jumped up and burst into the kitchen but as on the other night there was nothing. With the exception of ourselves, the place was empty. June just looked at me. 'We did hear that, didn't we?' she said. 'Yes,' was the only answer I could give her. 'Is this place haunted or something like that?' June asked. All along I thought I had an intruder but never for a minute did I think of a ghost!

As time moved on we became quite accustomed to hearing the 'ghost sounds', as we came to know them. We never at any time felt especially frightened of them but it was still weird, lying in the dark and hearing this thing walk all over the house and pulling out the chairs and table. By the way, there was never any *physical* evidence of the ghost. By this I mean the chair in the kitchen was never actually pulled out; it was just the sound of it moving that we heard.

Finally after about a year, June asked me to move into her place, as it was much bigger than mine. I agreed and left the noisy ghost behind at my old place. It was more than a year later that my boss approached me during my break and asked me a strange question out of the blue. 'Paul,' he said, 'When you rented that flat from me some time ago did you experience anything strange?'

'Like what?' I replied.

'I don't know. It's just the new tenants are complaining about hearing noises at night like someone walking about the place and moving furniture about.'

'Oh that's the ghost,' I replied. 'Tell them it's harmless and they will get used to it.'

My boss just laughed until I handed him my mobile and told him to ring June and ask her about it. I don't think he did ever tell them about the ghost but I am glad in one way that we were not the only ones to hear it.

DAVID, SOMERSET

My grandmother died on Mother's Day three years ago. A few days before she died, she was at home with my grandfather and began to feel unwell. She complained of a really bad headache and called my grandfather. She passed out and my grandfather called an ambulance. She was taken to the local hospital but she never regained consciousness. The doctors at the hospital said that she had had a massive brain haemorrhage and even if she had been at the hospital when it happened there was nothing that anyone would have been able to do. My mum and her family gathered and decided to have my grandmother removed from life support. She lingered until all her children gathered to say their final goodbyes and finally passed away on the evening of Mother's Day, 2004. There was only one person in the family who didn't get a chance to say goodbye; that was me.

I had moved to England to live and by the time I got things sorted out with my family and made my way back across to Ireland it was too late. I never made it to the hospital to say goodbye. I was sitting at my home in

England when my grandmother passed away and at the time she died I could smell her in my home. I know this sounds totally weird and mad but you know the smell of your grandmother's home? It's unique to her. Well, that's what I smelt. I knew there and then that she had died. Tears filled my eyes so much that my wife asked me what was wrong. I told her what I had just experienced. She phoned my family back in Ireland, who confirmed what I had told her. We both had a good cry that night.

When I did make it to Ireland for the funeral I talked to my mum about my experience. She began to cry and gave me a big hug as if I was her young little boy again. She said it must have been your grandmother wanting to say goodbye because you didn't get a chance to go to the hospital before she passed away. I felt like a total fool for not making more of an effort to see her before she passed away. I finally had a short chat with my grandma but wasn't sure if she heard me or not. I said that I was really sorry that I didn't get a chance to see her before she passed and that I missed her a whole lot. I hope she heard me and I know one day I will get to see her again.

ROSE, DUBLIN

My mum died of cancer in 1983. We had a very close family and my mum was more than just a parent to me; she was a friend to me. I had an especially close relationship with her, as I was her only daughter. My mother died very peacefully in our family home. She was surrounded by her loving family at the time of her passing. It was a very sad, heartbreaking time; yet I am glad that we were all there as she passed away. I have since bought my parents' house and have come to believe that the spirit of my mother is still there. Nothing truly remarkable has ever happened but there are times that footsteps can be heard when the house is empty. They make the sound of slippers gliding over carpet in the exact way they would if it was my mum who was walking around and occasionally stepping on a creaky floorboard. There are other occasions when her favourite perfume can be smelled in the air, despite the fact that the perfume is no longer used or kept in the house any more.

I've had several experiences in which I felt that Mum visited me at night as I slept. I remember on one such occasion, waking up from sleep to see her standing in the doorway of my room. She was wearing the bright flowered dress that she loved so much. I was surprised to see her, since my rational mind knew she was gone. I asked her what she was doing there. She told me that she just wanted to see her children again and make sure they were all right. I remember feeling her touch as she stroked my hair. I looked at the clock at the side of my bed; it was 3.46. I will always remember this time; it is engraved in my memory. I looked back at the door but Mum was gone, I rolled over in my bed and sobbed my heart out, crying that I didn't want her to go.

To this day the event seems so real but I will never be able to distinguish it from grief. It happened some time after her death. Since then, I've had two or three other very similar occurrences.

I've only recounted these experiences to one other person, my only living relative, my brother Stephen. I recall the day he came to visit me. We chatted about the normal stuff: kids, life and work. I picked up the courage to tell him about my experiences. I was shocked when he didn't call me nuts but instead told me about a similar experience he had, when Mum visited him in a dream and told him to take care of me, as we were all that was left and he was my elder and only brother. I am not sure if these occurrences are part of an ongoing grieving process that we are going through but I am fully certain that my mother is still looking after the both of us. I am a very sane, educated, professional person, as is my brother. To the best of my knowledge, these events are true.

MARY, COUNTY GALWAY

My sister and I have never been close. We always fought and hurt each other. As a result we grew up as strangers. This saddened our dad and when he died in 1991, it was with regret that he never saw Tania and me as friends. I did try to bury the hatchet with Tania over the years but when Tania has decided not to talk to you – that is that. I didn't have much contact either with her or with her husband for many years until one day I received a phone call from John, Tania's husband. He was ringing me to let me know that Tania was in hospital with cancer.

Even though we had fought like cats and dogs and had not spoken in years Tania was still my sister and I loved her very much. Tania's cancer was a very aggressive form that was eating its way through her system. Let's just say that over the next few months I saw my sister waste away as she lost her fight with cancer.

The night Tania died will stay with me for the rest of my life because I could feel the heart being ripped out of me as she passed away. She looked right at me in a moment of clarity and stated outright, 'I'm not going to die. I am *not* going to die!' I looked right back and said, 'Well, of course you're not going to die. We have a lot more fighting to do yet before I am finished with you. You're stuck with us.'

The night seemed to drag; time seemed to stand still. We took turns at a vigil at Tania's bed: myself, Mum and Tania's husband John. It was about 1.30 in the morning and at this point all three of us were at her bedside, when Tania asked me to take both her hands, which I did. Then she looked at Mum and said, 'Isn't she beautiful? Isn't she just beautiful?' Then she looked right into my eyes and said, 'I love you.' She had never said it before.

She thanked me for being there for her. She thanked me for being there for Mum. I remember a nurse came in to give Tania her medication. Tania just shook her head and said to the nurse, 'It's OK. I won't need them.' Because of the cancer Tania had become frail and weak but that night she squeezed my hand very tightly and took Mum's hand. She then looked deep into my eyes and said, 'It's time. Dad's here.'

That was the last thing Tania said to us. I looked over at Mum and asked her, 'Is she gone?' She replied, 'Yes.' That night Tania died; so did a part of me. There is an emptiness inside me that will never be filled. We lived almost thirty-five years as strangers. The night she died, we were sisters. We still are. Dad got his wish after all. I also learned a very valuable lesson that night: life is so short and you should live every day as if it is your last because one day it will be.

COLETTE, DUBLIN

I work for a legal firm in Dublin city centre. The office is a large converted Victorian house in the middle of a street full of the same type of offices. When I first came to the company, I was given an office on the third floor that was called the 'ghost room' by all the other staff. I was amused and thought nothing of it. I just passed it off as some kind of a joke on the new girl. However, after my first late night alone in the office, I changed my mind.

I was on my own in the office, working late preparing a case file for court. It was about 7.45 pm when I started to hear the slamming of doors in distant parts of the building. As I knew I was the only person in the building, I started quietly to panic. I cautiously opened my office door and called out to see if there was anyone there. No one answered but I heard the sound of a door near my office slam. I went out, umbrella in hand, and searched but I found no one.

I returned to my office, leaving the door open. That's when I heard the shuffling feet, the sound that slippers make on a carpet. The shuffling got louder and louder as it approached my office door, then faded down the hallway. My heart rate was soaring. I started to gather my papers together and I phoned my boyfriend to try and keep my sanity. I told him about the slamming doors, and, as I did so, the office door next to me slammed shut. My boyfriend also heard it over the phone. He told me to leave the office as there might be an intruder and that I should ring the Gardaí. I decided not to ring the Gardaí but as I left my office I heard a woman's laughter from the ceiling.

The next day at lunchtime, I plucked up the courage to tell the receptionist about my experiences, thinking that I had just had late-night heebie-jeebies. She looked at me quite seriously and called another employee over to hear my story. That employee nodded and said, 'Yep. The shuffling of feet, just like big slippers, right?' I discovered that other employees in the building had had the same experiences in the same areas. Other people had seen a woman's face in the kitchen window on the third floor.

Some time later, one of the junior solicitors had an experience that I am sure he will never forget. It was during another late-night rush. He was on the third floor using the photocopier in my office. I was in the boardroom on the lower floor. I heard him yell. I came running up to find him all pale and freaked out. He said that he was using the photocopier and that he heard someone call his name. He said the voice came from the kitchen area and when he looked up towards the kitchen window he saw the face of an old woman looking back at him.

Since then, I have joined the ranks of those who have heard the woman call their names. I now avoid the office at night. I don't know if my office is haunted by some deceased woman or not but I'm pretty sure there's something other than our staff members occupying this building.

BRIDGET, COUNTY MAYO

I grew up in a nice little part of Mayo called Mulranny. There was a family that lived across the road from me that had two brothers and three sisters. Two of the sisters were around my age and were my best friends. They were Susan and Rose. Tragically, both their parents were killed in a car crash. It was devastating for the family and the town. Susan and Rose were by then old enough and mature enough to take care of the rest of the family, with the help of their grandparents.

Anyway, one day I was visiting Susan and Rose when they asked me if I would mind their little brother while they went downtown to do some shopping. Their little brother was a dote and I was willing to mind him any time. So off they went.

There was nobody else in the house other than Edward, the little boy, and myself. I sat down on the sofa to read a magazine while Edward played in his playpen with his toys beside me. After about ten minutes I could hear the floorboards in the room above me creaking. It was like someone walking around the room. I then heard someone come down the stairs. I thought it might be Fiona, their other sister, but when I called out I got no reply. I waited for whoever it was to open the door and come in. Nothing happened. The sound of someone moving about went back up the stairs and I heard more creaking and banging around in the rooms above. I went upstairs and had a look around but there was nobody upstairs and all windows were secure. Yet I was sure of what I had heard.

I went back downstairs and sat back down on the sofa, purposefully leaving the door wide open. A few minutes later I heard creaking footsteps coming down the stairs and looked in the direction of the stairway. I couldn't see a thing. The noises continued until the sisters came back from shopping. I mentioned it to them and they were quite unsurprised. Seemingly the house had always been 'haunted', even while their parents were alive. This eased my mind a bit. From time to time I used to stay overnight when the sisters would invite me around for a chat late at night. I felt that they needed some company and did not much like being on their own.

On this particular night we had gone to bed as normal. I was in the downstairs bedroom and the sisters and their family were upstairs. That night I was woken up by the sound of a loud thud in the room. At first I wasn't sure where the noise came from but I was sure it came from within the room. I then became aware of someone or something sitting on the end of the bed watching me. I tried to move and scream but I could not. I just lay there trembling with fear. Then it stood up and made its way out of the room into the hallway but I don't remember the door of the bedroom opening or closing as it went out. Then all of a sudden the house alarm went off! That was it. I was convinced that there was an intruder in the house. The alarm woke the whole house up. The sisters came running down to see what was going on. I rang my dad, who was asleep in my house across the road.

When he came over he searched the whole house but found nothing: no windows or doors had been tampered with, nor was there anyone else in the house. I told them all what I had seen and felt in my bedroom just before the alarm went off. My dad was shocked but the sisters were not. I refused to go back into the bedroom and slept in the sisters' bedroom for the rest of the night but I did not sleep much. It was later on the next day that Susan told me that what I had experienced in that room was experienced by her parents several times, as that was their bedroom when they were alive. I tried to take all this in. But why then did the alarm go off? We called the alarm company to get it checked out and they found no fault with it.

ANN, COUNTY KILKENNY

My mother died suddenly in June, 1990, a week before her fortieth birthday. In an instant my whole life changed. Coupled with the horrible grief I was experiencing at losing my mother, my closest friend, the company that I worked for announced that it was closing and I was faced with unemployment. I was left alone in the house and in life. Although my grandparents lived close by they seemed a million miles away when I walked into my empty house at night. My world had fallen down around me. In the two years before my mother's death, she developed cancer and subsequently had severe mental breakdowns from which she never recovered. She had just come through the heartache of a broken marriage and being abused by a drunken husband, sadly my father. My life was now such that I was a bundle of nerves filled with grief and stress.

The first event in my house happened two weeks after my mother's funeral. Stephen, an old friend of mine, and I were reunited after nearly two years of not speaking to each other – the only light in the pit of blackness I felt I was living in. It was not rare for him to stay over after a night of talking, crying, and catching up on the time we had spent away from each other. One Sunday morning Stephen paid a visit to me after going to Mass. Stephen is a devout Catholic. On this occasion he was accompanied by Noel, a good friend of his, whom I had met only once before. We began talking and laughing, and ended up sitting out in the back garden having an early Sunday lunch. It seemed like a great morning.

Then all a sudden Stephen announced 'Well, aren't you going to see what she wants?'

'What are you talking about?' I asked, confused.

'Your grandmother is in the house. She just called for you.'

I immediately got up from where I was sitting and went into the house. It was not strange to me that my grandmother would have been in my house unannounced since she had a key but she always called me first to let me know she was popping over. I was quite surprised when I found no one there. I checked the entire house, calling my grandmother's name, and then went back out into the garden with an odd look on my face and explained to both Stephen and Noel that there was absolutely no one other than the three of us in the house. Stephen said that he was sure that he heard my grandmother calling me. Noel also said that he heard my name being called. I went to the phone to call my grandmother. She immediately answered her phone. I explained the situation to her, and she laughed it off, saying that the voice they heard must have come from my neighbours.

I was more confused than ever but not really bothered by the situation. I went back into the garden to give the guys an update on my conversation. Stephen immediately went pale and said, 'There was somebody in this house. There was a voice. It was calling your name. It was a woman and it was not your grandmother. I suggest we search your house.'

'I've already looked and there is no one here!' I protested.

Noel piped up, 'I don't know you very well but I know what I just heard. There was a woman in this house and she was calling your name. I still can't get over the fact that you didn't hear it because it was very loud and came from the vicinity of your kitchen.'

Hoping to ease the situation I replied, 'Look, it must have come from the neighbours. So let's all forget about it. No harm done.' Stephen, looking very nervous and scared, said again that he had definitely heard the voice and that it came from inside the house – not from neighbours, a good distance away. Noel was extremely nervous and expressed his desire to leave. After some further discussion and my trying to calm everyone's nerves, Stephen agreed to drop Noel home. They left and I went back to my everyday activities. I didn't giving it much more thought until two Sundays later.

It was afternoon and I was on the phone with a good friend named Karen. I was sitting in my recliner located in the living room. I was chatting away quite happily about a party we were planning at my house for the following Saturday. All of a sudden I heard a woman's voice saying something from the adjoining kitchen. I dropped the phone, jumped out of my chair, and ran into the kitchen shouting, 'Who's there?' There was no answer: no one was there. The kitchen door was still latched and my house was silent. My grandparents were away for the afternoon visiting relatives. I went back to the phone and said, 'You will never believe what just happened.'

'Who's there?' Karen asked.

'No one,' I replied. 'There isn't anyone here.'

'I just heard a woman call out your name,' she said. Feeling a little relieved that I was not losing my mind I told her that I had heard it too. I asked her if she heard what was said but she could only say that it sounded like my mother or my grandmother. 'There's nobody in the house except me,' I repeated.

Karen then gave me the best advice possible at the time. She said, 'Get out of the house.' I hung up the phone as quickly as possible. I was very much afraid.

I rang Stephen and asked him if I could pop over. He could tell that there was something wrong by the tone of my voice. He agreed and I left straight away. I stayed with Stephen the whole afternoon. I thought that I might be having a mental breakdown myself. Yet the fact that Karen heard the voice ruled that one out. I knew that the voice came from my kitchen and, yes, it sounded like my mother or grandmother.

Later on that day I rang my grandparents and I told them about the situation. My grandfather, a gentle man who was badly affected by my mother's death, listened up to the part where I said it sounded like my mother's voice. He told me that it was all in my mind and that I should return home and try to forget about it. My grandmother said nothing. I went home. I cautiously walked in and for a while I was too scared to make a sound, still trying to piece together in my mind what had happened and looking for a viable explanation. At one point, I opened all the windows and drapes, turned on the television and tried to make things as cheery as possible in the house. After all, it *was* my house. It helped a little but I slept with the light on for the next few nights.

The next few weeks were relatively quiet, until one day I came home to find the place a mess. All my clothes were flung about the place. Another morning I went into my kitchen and I was quite shocked to find the entire room covered with at least an inch of baking soda. I stood and stared at the floor for what must have been half an hour. The door was locked. No one had been able to get inside. The next day, I had all the locks to my house changed (I possessed the only key), locked all the windows and vowed to face my problem with a new resolve. I was going to figure out whatever was going on. I was determined to find a rational explanation for these incidents.

It was about this time that all hell broke loose. Lights flashed and doors opened and slammed closed. My stereo was on and I heard whispering and laughter. A few pieces of jewellery that had gone missing showed up out of nowhere. I could set something down, turn around for two seconds and it would vanish only to turn up later in some other place in the house. There is no doubt in my mind that no one was able to get into the house. The television still turned itself on in the middle of the night. My clothes would be mysteriously spread on the floor of my whole house, still on the hangers. My friends were sure that the house was haunted. Needless to say, they gradually stopped coming by.

On the other hand, Stephen was my rock. He did not stop coming over, although he spent many restless nights in the house. He once woke me in the middle of the night insisting that someone had opened the bedroom door, crossed the room and gone into the closet. Stephen bought me a cat to keep me company on the nights he could not stay over. She was very affectionate but she too sensed that things were not right in my house. On many an occasion she would hiss at the wall or arch her back at an empty doorway and she would track empty air with her eyes.

I began to realise myself that my house was in fact haunted – but by whom? The obvious person who came to mind was my mother. She had died suddenly and was troubled by mental illness beforehand. I spoke to my local priest about my situation and asked if he would bless my house. He agreed. I spoke to him about the possibilities of a haunting and said that I was concerned that my mother was not at rest. It did help somewhat that he, having known my mother personally, had no doubts that my mother was now in peace. He assured me that everything would be fine.

I still was not convinced that the spirit in my house wasn't my mother. After all, it was her voice that so many of us heard. A few nights later the parish priest came over and performed a blessing on the house and on myself. The house seemed to settle down for a while after this but the disturbances started again. I could take no more of it. Stephen and I had now become serious in our relationship so I moved in with him permanently.

I eventually packed up everything that I wanted to bring. I sold off most of the furniture that remained in the house. On the final day that I left that house, I went to close the front door and lock it. I felt a sense of loss looking at the empty house. I was angry and sad to leave my childhood home, thinking of all the memories it held for me. I said goodbye to the empty house. Since then Stephen and I have married and have two children of our own, two girls. I often think back to those troublesome days and wonder what on earth it was that drove me from my family home.

ANGELA, COUNTY GALWAY

We lived for a number of years in an old cottage on the main Galway-Dublin road, just a few miles outside Galway. When I was alone in the house during the day, I always had the feeling that someone was watching me. A few months after we moved in, my two little girls and I were alone waiting for my husband to come home for dinner. The girls ran from our living room into the bedroom where I was folding clothes, shouting that they had seen a ghost. At first, I thought they had seen a real man in the back yard and that frightened me more than the idea of a ghost but they insisted that they had seen a tall, white figure in the middle of our living room. I chalked it up to active imaginations and let it go at that, although I did mention it to their father that night.

The next night we went out with some friends and left the girls with a reliable babysitter. When we returned, all the lights were on in the house. As we walked up the path I could see in through the sitting-room window. Standing in the front room was an old man, balding, with a round face!

I saw him clearly for a split second – then told my husband. We first thought it was a friend of the babysitter. My husband thought the man was inside the house and was very concerned. We went straight into the sitting room to speak to the man we had just seen standing there but when we went into the room he was gone. We called out for the babysitter and she came in from the kitchen that was located at the rear of the building. I asked where the girls were and she said they were in bed. I enquired a who the man was in the sitting room. She shook her and said, 'I don't know,' and said that she and the ch had been the only ones in the house all night. My husband searched the house and the rear garden but found nothing. Still very confused and nervous, I mentioned to the sitter what I had just seen.

She said, 'Oh, no!' The girls had a really hard time falling asleep that night! They kept telling me that an old man was looking at them through the window! I freaked out. I saw him inside and the girls had seen him outside looking in at them! We then called the Gardaí, who came around quite quickly. I explained the situation to them and they did a cursory search of the grounds. Before they left one of the Gardaí said that the house had had a history of unexplained happenings as long as he could remember and he had been stationed there for quite a number of years.

Next day, I called the parish priest and asked to have the house blessed. That weekend he came and blessed everything and we never saw the old man again!

VAL, COUNTY ANTRIM

Ever since I can remember I have had to have a light on in my bedroom when I go to bed at night. This is as a result of my childhood fear of the dark. I'm nearly fifty now and my husband of twenty-five years has adjusted to always having a light on at night. We have two sons, one now aged nineteen and the other seventeen.

We had just moved into a three-storey townhouse. My husband and I occupied the top floor, which consisted of a bedroom, a large dressing room and a bathroom. The stairs entered in the middle so you could walk the whole floor in a circle. At the time my two sons had the rooms right below us and from there you could easily hear when someone was walking around on the top floor. Below them were the sitting room and kitchen.

One night after we had been in bed for a couple of hours, I was still awake in bed watching television as I always do because I don't like falling asleep in a dark room. All of a sudden I heard someone walk up the stairs and in a loud whisper call my name. I thought it was one of my children so I sat up and replied in a loud whisper so as not to wake my husband. But no one answered.

Worried that something was wrong with one of the kids, I got up and went downstairs and checked on both of them in turn. They were sound asleep. Odd, I thought. I went back upstairs to bed and just a few minutes later I heard from the stairs my name being called again in a loud whisper. I *froze*. I knew it wasn't my kids. I had just checked on them. I didn't move; I just lay there frozen. Eventually I started to poke my husband under the covers to wake him up and the noises stopped. I let my husband sleep and just lay there frozen for about an hour till I finally fell asleep.

The next morning while I was telling my husband about what had happened, my elder son walked in and asked, 'What was going on upstairs last night? From my room it sounded like someone stomping their way all around the rooms upstairs.' He had heard the footsteps too. What a relief that was to me! I told him the story of what happened that night and I tell you we all felt pretty spooked. This continued night after night. Even my husband heard it. We searched the house every time we heard the footsteps but found nothing. The family was in deep discussions about these strange happenings – everyone except for my younger son, who at the time was only thirteen years of age and was not talking much about it. I initially thought that all this was scaring him – until one day while the boys were in school I was changing their bedclothes and I found what I now know to be an Ouija board in my youngest son's bedroom.

That evening I confronted him with it and asked him what was going on. He broke down, sobbing. He said it was all a game with him and his friends. That they did not believe in it and just started to play with it. It turned out that the board belonged to one of his friends and that it was kept in my home so it would not be found. He said that while playing with it they made contact with a man who said his name was Martin and that Martin used to answer any questions they asked.

It all started to make sense to me then. The footsteps we were hearing moving around the house were the spirit of this Martin. I did not know what to do. I rang the only person I could think of who might help, the local priest. He came around and I told him the whole story – all about this Martin and how he managed to make his way into my home. He said that he would bless the house and all of us. We all heard a Mass together and he made his way around the house, blessing every room.

Then the priest asked me to light the fire. This I thought strange, as it was a hot summer, but light it I did. He took the Ouija board and said a prayer as he put the board into the fire. We all watched it burn. He said that all our troubles should now be gone. He also warned my son never to play with anything like that again, that it was the devil's work and to stay away from it. It must have worked for Martin never came again, thank goodness.

TRACEY, COUNTY DUBLIN

I grew up in a house with something in it. I'm not sure if it was a ghost or something else but strange things happened all the time.

I thought this experience was the most frightening thing ever. My mum and dad had gone to Cork for a long weekend break. My grandmother was staying with us while they were gone. It was a bright sunny day around 11 am. My grandmother and brother were in the utility room getting a picnic set ready. We were planning to go to the park later for a picnic. I was in the kitchen making some sandwiches and rolls. My parents never shut the door to their room and a large marble statue held the door open.

All of a sudden the front door of the house opened and slammed shut. My grandmother and brother could see a dark figure in the doorway. They thought it was my dad but never wondered why he was there and not in Cork. Then the person stomped down the hallway. I heard him come in and saw the figure go by me and I also thought it was my dad. I did not get a close look. The person stomped though the house to my parents' bedroom. Then we heard the marble statue being pushed and their bedroom door slam shut. A little while later my grandmother came into the kitchen and said, 'Has Kathleen (my mother) come in?' I said 'No.'

Grandma said, 'They must have had a fight the way your dad stomped through the house.'

We went outside to find my mum. Their car was not there. Grandma said, 'Kathleen must have been so mad she left.' We went inside to talk to my dad. We went to the bedroom and the door was shut and locked. We knocked on the door. 'Dad, let us in. What is wrong?' No answer. We kept on trying to get the door open but it would not move. We eventually did get it open but there was nobody in the room at all.

This freaked my grandmother out. She said, 'Something is wrong.' She said that she needed to contact somebody – my parents (her daughter). She rang my mother's mobile phone only to find out that my dad had passed away from a heart attack earlier that day. We believe that we did see Dad standing in the doorway and stomping into his bedroom. I have heard of loved ones paying a final visit to say goodbye but never in a violent angry way like this. I don't know the meaning of this and might never know. But I do know that Dad came back to the house the day he died.

EMILY, COUNTY OFFALY

My mother lived in a house that was built by her father in the late 1920s. It was built on the side of a hill where there had been an old cottage dating back to the early 1800s. My grandparents also lived with us in this house. In 1942 my grandfather died and in 1948 my grandmother died. There are no other records of any deaths in the house other than these.

It was not until 1987 that I began to experience strange happenings in the house. I slept in my own bedroom, which used to be my grandparents' room. I don't know if I was dreaming this at the time but during the night, my bed was pushed and a voice said, 'Why are you in my house?' I replied, 'Because I belong here.' Whatever it was left the room.

One Friday night I was having some friends in for a

sleep-over. My mother was in the kitchen making some popcorn as we had rented a video for the night. We were all having a great time when all of a sudden we heard footsteps coming down the stairs. I went to the staircase, turned on the light and no one was there. I went upstairs and looked through all the rooms but I could see nothing. I went back downstairs and our conversations continued but this time I left the living room door open to observe the staircase. We were all talking and again the footsteps started down the steps. A female voice said, 'Tom, it's time for bed.' I got up and looked up the staircase and no one was there but the hallway and staircase were cold. I looked at the clock and it was 11.50 pm, which on normal nights was past my bedtime.

I looked at my mum, who was now standing with tears in her eyes. I asked what was wrong. She replied, 'Nothing' and just brushed the tears from her eyes. I asked who was calling the name 'Tom'. You see, Tom was my grandfather's name. This was, needless to say, unsettling. I tried to put it to the back of my mind but the other girls would not. They kept asking if my house was haunted, I replied 'No! Don't be silly.' They begged me to have a séance. I agreed, to shut them up, so we all gathered in a circle in my bedroom holding hands, giggling away at the fact that we were about to have a séance.

Well, brave hearts that we were, we began. We used the old cliché: tap once for yes and twice for no, but when we asked if the house was haunted, we heard a loud tap on the bedroom floor and the hallway light went out. We all screamed. This alerted Mum that something was up. She came into the room asking what was going on. I could never lie to Mum so I told her what we were up to.

She just laughed and said 'Right. Bedtime, all of you.' She smiled and said, 'Nothing can hurt you,' and repeated that we should go to bed.

A few nights later Mum and I were in the sitting room when we heard someone moving at the top of the stairs. We went to investigate but when I reached the top of the stairs it was ice cold and I immediately thought, 'OK. Here we go. It's too hot for it to be this cold.' I turned around and saw a shadow of a woman literally walk into my bedroom. I looked at Mum and she was looking at me as if to say, 'Did you just see that?' The shadow turned, looked at me and disappeared. The hallway became hot and that night I slept in Mum's room.

I felt compelled to go to the grave of my grandmother. There I asked her if it was she who was haunting the house. I told her that if it was she who was doing it she was frightening us and I asked her to stop. I can only assume that it was she as we never again heard anything or saw anything on the stairs.

ISABELLA, COUNTY DUBLIN

This odd occurrence took place in early January 2003. I was at my grandparents' house during the Christmas holidays. They live in Bantry, County Cork, in a rather grand house that they bought cheaply, because of its derelict state. Now it has been restored to pristine condition, with the décor resembling a late-18th-century castle.

The first night I stayed in the house there were no disturbances but on the second night I woke up to the sound of a woman screaming and banging on a door. I cautiously opened my bedroom door and peered over the banister. The sound was coming from the entrance hall that was just below. I continued to hear the sound but I could see nobody. The sound was coming from inside the house, not outside. At first I thought it was a joke but both my grandparents were asleep. I got spooked and returned to my bedroom, where I lay awake until the sound eventually ceased.

When I woke the next morning, I told my grandfather what I had experienced. He passed it off as a dream but it was evident from the look on his face that he was hiding something. Later that day I called my parents back home. We had the usual chatter about nothing and everything and I decided to ask them if at any time they had ever heard strange noises when they stayed over at my grandparents' house. My mum said they would explain it all when I got home. This made me even more curious and I was determined to find out what was going on.

I heard the same sound several times during my stay there but my grandparents simply refused to acknowledge that anything was happening. When I returned home I insisted that my parents tell me everything that had gone on at my grandparents' home. It turned out that before my grandparents bought the house it had been destroyed in a fire and the lady of the house was burned to death. She tried to make her escape through the front door but it was locked. She did not realise that all the rest of the family had made it to safety via the rear of the building. They could hear her banging on the door and screaming for help but it was too late: the fire spread through the whole house. She died in the entrance hall.

Ever since I heard this story, I have been fascinated with the spirit world and love spending time at my grandparents' house.

NATHAN, COUNTY WESTMEATH

It was in the autumn/early winter of 2005 that I had the weirdest experience I've ever had. I'm not a believer in the supernatural but since this happened I have been willing to give it a bit more credence.

I was driving through Maynooth, heading back to Mullingar from Dublin. . It was in mid-October: I can't be specific about the date. It was the middle of the night practically, around 1.30 am. I was driving along the long winding two-lane pitch-dark road when all of a sudden a boy ran out in front of the car on to the road. I was sure I had hit him. There was no way of stopping in time. I was probably doing about forty-five or fifty miles per hour. As I locked my brakes my car skidded for some distance. I got out of my car and ran back to where I felt I had hit the boy and where I definitely saw him but there was nobody there at all. I got my torch from the boot of my car and searched the nearby fields to see if he was there – but nothing. I even checked the front of my car. Nothing – not even a scratch. It was too weird.

I resumed my journey but could not get the incident out of my head. So I turned my car around and returned to Maynooth, where I reported the incident in the Garda station. The Garda on duty stopped me talking and asked me to describe the little boy. This I did. He then told me a story about the ghost of a little boy who had been seen running across the road, on that exact same spot, on many occasions and had been reported to his station. I suddenly got this sense of fright jolting up through me as I started to realise that I had just seen a ghost. The Garda took all my details on the off-chance that it was not the ghost of the little boy but he assured me that it was. I did not drive that road again that night but went the long way home through Portarlington.

SARA, COUNTY WEXFORD

My brother was killed in a car accident in 1998. We were a very close family and this accident that took Brian away from us devastated my parents and me. Over the years, since my brother Brian passed away, I have managed to get over his death. I have always had the feeling that he is nearby. If I am alone in the bedroom reading or listening to music, I will catch a glimpse of someone passing by the open door. Or if I am in the living room, I will see someone standing in the dining room, leaning against the doorpost to the living room. Every time it is a tall, thin figure dressed in white T-shirt and dark jeans. This is what my brother was wearing the night he was killed. I have also caught the smell of his cologne.

There have also been times when I am just about to fall asleep and I feel the edge of the bed sink, as if someone is sitting on the edge or leaning on it. I know it is not my husband as he is on the other side of me with his back to me. Sometimes I wake up at night with the feeling of someone stroking my hair. I know it is not my husband. It was in 2005 that I got my biggest shock and a true sense that Brian is still around me. My son was almost five. When he was born I named him after my brother. I told my brother Brian in my mind's prayer that I was naming the baby after him. There are times when my son will be watching television or playing while I'm cleaning up in another room. I'll come in to check on him and he'll say, 'Hi.' Then he'll look around and say, 'You frightened my friend away. Where is he?'

I never paid much attention to this until one day I was giving my son a bath and he asked about his friend. I asked him, 'What friend?' He kept asking, 'Where did he go?' When he was dressed, he went through the dining room to go into the living room, where his dad was. My son stopped by the table where I have framed family pictures displayed. He pointed at the one of my brother and said excitedly, 'There he is. There's the friend.' I took the picture down and handed it to my son. He pointed to my brother and said, 'Yep, that's him.' Then he went into the living room to watch a movie before bed.

When my son is playing in his room and I hear him talking to his friend I always get very upset inside for I know in my heart who is playing with him and who is still looking after his little sister. I couldn't think of a better guardian angel for my son than my brother.

DOMINIC, COUNTY KILDARE
You would think that a flat built in late 1990s where my wife and I are the first tenants would be an unusual location to experience ghostly phenomena – but that's what we have. We have had the usual stuff: things that I put down go missing and turn up days later; a spate of light bulbs blowing; and the occasional barely audible voice. But then things started to build up even more strongly over a

period of some weeks. It became so strong that we are now beginning to see what we feel are actual manifestations.

Things don't seem to be evil or malevolent but our cat often looks at things we can't see. The main thing we feel is a presence near our bedroom door. Basically it's just a shadowy figure about 5ft tall. Both my wife and I feel that it gives an impression of being female. All it seems to do is watch us while we're sleeping. It doesn't seem to want to harm us but it makes us feel uncomfortable.

Then there is the black shape that passes our living room door heading to the front door of the flat. This other shadow is not the same one as up in the bedroom as this one seems to give off the feeling that it is male. I have had this experience many times.

Who these figures are we can't explain. They do not appear to be deceased family members or friends who have gone on. We have carried out some research and there were not, according to the records, any previous buildings on the site. Who or what these apparitions are we do not know but over many years we have become accustomed to their sharing our flat with us. They have never harmed us or made us feel unwelcome, so we are happy to continue on as we are at present.

ANDREW, DUBLIN

About seven years ago I worked the night shift at a homeless shelter in Dublin city. Weird things sometimes happened in and around the shelter. My office was a converted sitting room that was part of one of the many buildings joined together to make up the whole complex. I always felt as if there was someone in the room watching me.

There was a room in one of the wings where the door refused to stay open. It would close mostly with force, yet had no spring attached. When I had to clean that room I always put a chair against the door to keep it open; otherwise the door would slam. It didn't matter if all the windows were closed. One night I was doing my rounds. No one was awake. I went through the swinging doors from the main corridor that led to the central hallway and felt someone brush past me. There was absolutely no one there except me.

On another night I was in the office as one of the residents was up quite late. From my office I could see right down the main corridor. I got a strange feeling that someone was watching me (you know that weird feeling you get). I looked up along the corridor but just as I did I saw the swing doors open and close, as if someone had just walked through them. (I must point out that there are glass panels in the doors to enable you to see through them). My heart was going a mile a minute. I started sleeping in the childcare room after that.

Another night I was sitting in my office when the radio suddenly came on. It made me jump and almost scream out. I switched it off, lay back down and started to relax when it turned itself on again and the music started playing. I got up and checked it and the music turned itself off as I got near. This time I unplugged the radio but when I lay back down I couldn't sleep. I stared at the ceiling, thinking how weird it was: the radio playing music and turning itself on and off.

As I was looking up at the ceiling, I saw a bright white dot of light suddenly come through the ceiling and float down and over to the side of the room where the radio was. I remember thinking that the light was very white and clear. As I watched, the dot of light floated above the radio, then away from it. It rose and went out through one of the windows. I really didn't quite believe it. You can imagine that I was nervous at work after that and I could not wait for the day shifts to swing back around.

Later on that night, it was time for me to do my rounds. I had to leave the office to do that. I went out into the foyer and had to go through the swing doors connecting the foyer to the central hall that I had seen swinging open and closed earlier on. I hesitated just at the doors because I started to feel that sense of menace again and, as I watched, the door began to move all by itself. I was alone in the shelter. I hopped right back into the office and locked myself in. My heart was slamming in my chest. I was so frightened that I was sweating and I felt faint.

When the day-time staff member reported for duty he found me locked in the office and thought this was very strange. A while after these happenings I was chatting with another staff member, when I picked up the courage to tell him about what I was experiencing. I was half-expecting him to start laughing and calling me stupid or mad but he didn't. He said, 'Thank you. I have also experienced weird stuff but was too afraid to say anything about it.' I felt some sort of relief that I was not the only person to experience the strange happenings at the home but this did not make me feel any safer working there. I soon changed my job and am all the better for it. I now am a firm believer in the paranormal and would not ever wish such frightening experiences on anyone.

SARAH, COUNTY CORK

Twenty years ago we lived in Cork City. Our flat was a compact little flat but it served our needs. It was part of a large flat complex. There had never been anything built on the location before the flats, as far as I know. The only real problem was that the flats had a bad drainage system. When it rained heavily our flat sometimes flooded. We were not the first tenants to live there. It had been briefly occupied by another family before we bought it. One of them was dying of cancer, so they had decided to move back home to County Wicklow to be closer to their family.

We were given permission from the complex owners to carry out some light construction work. This was to make the space a little larger for us. It was around then that I had the weirdest experiences. One night I was lying in bed next to my husband. I had my eyes closed but I wasn't asleep. Then I felt a hand caress my face. I opened my eyes to look at my husband and his back was turned to me. I sat up in the bed but he was fast asleep. I woke him and told him what had happened but he said I was dreaming and that I should go back to sleep. So I lay back down and tried to go to sleep, but I was frightened by it.

Another night, shortly after this, I was trying to go back to sleep and my arm was hanging off the side of the bed. Suddenly I felt a cold presence by my hand and then I felt something touch my hand as if it were holding it. I snatched my hand up on to the bed, hid it under the covers and rolled over so I was facing the floor and the doorway to the bedroom. As I did this I could hear someone giggling, as if they were enjoying seeing me scared. I tried to focus on the room with the limited light coming in through the bedroom window. I had a bedside lamp but I was too scared to reach out to switch it on. As I searched the room with my eyes I saw a dot of bright white light floating through the wall of my son's room. It floated toward me and then right past my bed and out the window.

I never told anyone, not even my husband. I thought I must have been going crazy. I don't know how my unit could have been haunted at all. It was only four years old when we bought it and no one ever died there. Nor had anything ever been built there before. Over the next few months I experienced similar things in the flat but only by myself. I slowly put the idea into my husband's mind that I did not like the flat and would prefer if we lived somewhere else. It took a while but I did manage to get out of that flat. I do not know what on earth it was but it scared the life out of me and changed my attitude to the paranormal.

JESSICA, COUNTY CLARE

I inherited my grandmother's house after she died in 1992. She died suddenly in her sleep. She went peacefully without any pain. The house was not left to me or anything like that. It was just a case that all other family members had their own houses and I was living in a flat with my husband and family. So everyone felt that I should have it. The house had remained untouched since my grandmother died so when I moved in during the month of November that year, I had to clear out all my grandmother's furniture and her clothes. They still filled the wardrobe and dressers. Eager to make the house our own, we set about cleaning out the house and refurbishing it to our liking.

That's when the trouble started. The first thing we experienced was a loud thumping noise coming from the kitchen area, which at first we dismissed as noisy plumbing. Then there were some other strange things. Lights would be switched on by unseen hands while we were out of the house. We tried to take these curious occurrences in our stride but it was when we hung a picture of my family on the wall that I began to realise that something weird was really going on in this house. The morning after hanging it we found it on the floor, neatly propped against the wall. At first we thought it had merely fallen off the nail, so we re-hung it. In fact, five times we tried to hang the picture and each time it was taken down and set against the wall.

In 1993 we started to redecorate the main bedroom; the poltergeist activity increased. Throughout the day we stripped the old wallpaper off the walls and got it ready for redecorating but as we did this we were both (my husband and I) unnerved by the sensation of being watched. That night crashing noises and loud banging could be heard coming from the main bedroom. My husband went to investigate but when he entered the room all the banging stopped. He returned to the room that we were sleeping in, saying that every thing was as we had left it. He then jokingly said, 'It must be your grandmother; maybe she does not like the new wallpaper.'

I did not find this funny as I began to think he might be right – about my grandmother, not the wallpaper. The next day I went to see my mother and told her the full story about the weird happenings at my grandmother's old place. I thoughts she was going to tell me a fabulous story about why all this was happening to me and the house. But no. She just shrugged her shoulders and said, 'I have no idea what's happening in the house.'

The last straw came later that year. It was in the early hours of the night when I was woken up by the sound of my son screaming out for me. Both my husband and I ran into his bedroom to find him almost sitting up on the headboard in sheer terror. We brought him from his bedroom into ours and managed to calm him down. At first we thought he might have had a nightmare but he told us that he woke up thinking that one of us had come into his room and was sitting on the end of his bed. He could feel someone sitting there but when he looked down all he could see was a black shadow looking at him. It was at this point that he started to scream out. He also said that just before we entered the room the shadow stood up and vanished. From that moment on he refused to sleep in that room.

We were now desperate for help and turned to our parish priest. We spoke to him about what was going on in the house and he agreed to perform a blessing on the house. He did this in April 1993: he said a prayer in every room of the house, then we all prayed in the sitting room and said a special prayer for my grandmother. It was during this prayer that I remember quietly saying to myself, 'If this is you, Gran, please stop. I can't take it any more.' I am glad to say that since that day nothing out of the ordinary has happened. I don't know if it was the spirit of my Gran or something else that the priest cleared the house of but I am grateful that it is over.

JENNA, COUNTY KILKENNY

My parents' house in Kilkenny was a very haunted house. As far as I can remember we never felt alone in the house. You always knew someone or something was watching you. From a very early age, both my sister and I knew that there was something just not right around the place. I remember when I was about fifteen years old (I am now twenty-eight) and I was standing in my bedroom combing my hair in the mirror, when I saw someone who I thought was my mother walk past my bedroom into her bedroom. This I felt strange, as she did not seem to notice that I was there or even say, 'Hi!' I followed her into her room but she was not there. In fact, there was nobody there. This freaked me out a little but when I returned to my room I remember feeling that something was in the room with me, watching me. At the time there was only one person, my sister, in the house with me and she was downstairs watching television. My sister and I both refused to go upstairs alone, and up to the age of ten or so we had always made somebody stand at the bottom of the stairs to watch us while we went to the bathroom, with the door open.

My mother also said that when I was two or three I had an imaginary friend named Rachel. I constantly played with Rachel up in my bedroom, sometimes into the early hours of the morning. Suddenly I stopped talking about Rachel and my mother asked me why.

I replied, 'She died.' Now we both wonder whether 'Rachel' was really imaginary or a ghost.

One day my mum was out the back hanging out the washing. She was looking up at my bedroom, shouting my name. I answered her from the kitchen. She looked at me strangely. She asked who was up in my room as I was in the kitchen. I went to check and there was nobody. I opened my bedroom window and shouted down that there was nobody up here at all. My parents still live in the same house and even to this day when I pop over to visit I dislike going upstairs to use the bathroom.

GABRIELLA, DUBLIN

About three years ago, I rented an apartment in the Rathmines area of Dublin. Most of my neighbours were sound except for one neighbour. He said that his bathroom was haunted and that once when he was taking a bath he was confronted by a sinister and angry man. He said that the man disappeared just as quickly as he appeared. Prior to his living there, a woman and her daughter lived there and the daughter was afraid of the bathroom and wouldn't go in there when it was dark. Apparently one night while she was taking a bath a bottle that was on the windowsill flew across the room and smashed on the floor as if someone had thrown it. The window was not open, so it couldn't have been the wind.

I felt at first that this guy was just trying to scare me a little. That was until my own experiences. One evening I was awakened from my sleep by the noise of people arguing just outside my apartment door. I peeped out through the security spyglass but saw nothing, nobody. Yet I could still hear them. I felt safe enough to open the door as I could see nobody there. When I did, the arguing stopped.

Another night I was sitting in the living-room area of the apartment watching television. I thought I heard someone at the front door so I turned the sound down on the television. It was then that I heard footsteps coming up from the front door and into my bedroom, yet I could see nothing. I rushed into my bedroom expecting to see someone but there was nothing: the whole apartment was empty except for me.

A few days later I bumped into the guy who told me the story about his bathroom. I felt safe telling him about my experiences as they were no stranger than his and at least I knew he wouldn't think I was mad. I was glad I did as he went on to tell me loads about the building. He also said that my apartment never stayed occupied for long periods. He said people just upped and left without saying anything. He said that the whole place was haunted and he suspected that it was haunted by the spirits of a family that had once lived there. Before it was converted into apartments this was an individual house.

This was not doing my nerves any good. I did not like the idea of living in a haunted place. That day I packed up my stuff and joined the many before me who just left the apartment. I returned to my parents' house looking for my old room back. They laughed, saying, 'Only a few weeks in the real world and you're back!' That was until I told them why.

CHRISTINA, DUBLIN

When my husband and I got married, we rented this house for a short period while we were waiting for our own house to be finished. It was the usual situation: we were buying a new house and we sold our old one. We had to move out of our home for the new owners to move in, so we rented for a short time.

We lived in the house from April 2000 until August 2000. It was a small brick house, with two bedrooms, a bath and an upstairs loo. We used the spare bedroom to store boxes containing all the belongings we did not need every day. About a week after we moved in, my husband and I would hear talking downstairs when we were going to bed. When we went down to see who it was, the talking would stop and there was nobody there. We just let it go. About a week later, I was upstairs making the bed when I heard someone coming up the stairs. At first I thought it was my husband home from work but when I called out his name there was no reply. When I went to investigate, the house was empty. But that's not all.

My sister and her husband came over for a meal one night and they brought a bottle of wine. I placed the wine on the kitchen counter while I finished cooking the meal. We were chatting in the sitting room when we heard a crash in the kitchen. When we went into the kitchen we found the bottle of wine smashed on the kitchen floor. I know that I did not place it on the edge of the counter but had put it well in on the counter. There was no way that it accidentally slipped off the counter. Anyway, the bottle of wine became the talking point of the evening so I decided to tell them about the other happenings. They both started slagging us, going, 'Ooooo! Who has a ghost?!' We all just laughed.

About a week after this my sister called one evening and said that she needed to talk to me. I noticed that when they were leaving and saying goodnight at the front door she had looked into my house and then straight at me. I knew that she had seen something and when I asked her what was wrong she just said, 'Nothing! Must be what we were talking about all night playing tricks in my mind.' She said goodnight and left. Nothing else had happened that night but a week later I got the phone call from my sister asking me how long I had left there before we moved into our new house. I said, 'Not long now; why?' She told me that when she was leaving our house after the dinner she thought she saw or did see – she is not sure – the shadow of a man standing in the kitchen. She said he was there one second and gone the next. After that we put pressure on the builders to get the new house finished.

In August 2000 we moved into our new home and I have to say it felt great. The house was big, spacious and bright. All was going great for us. We had left the weirdness of the old house behind us – or so we thought. Soon after we moved in, doors used to open after they had been locked and bolted for the night. Lights would turn on and the room would go from hot to freezing. We would all get goose bumps at the same time for no apparent reason. At first we thought it was teething problems with a new house but after we had the builders check everything out and had been told that nothing was wrong with the electrics, we did start to worry. After this the radio in the kitchen would come on by itself during the night. My husband had to go down several times to switch it off until one night in rage he threw it into the bin. Then the thing moved its attention to the television. The channels would change as if by themselves. At first my husband thought it was me. On one occasion he started to argue, asking why I had changed the channel while he was watching a particular programme? I said it was not me, telling him he had the remote, and sure enough it was on the floor beside him.

One of our most recent experiences was with the family pictures on the fireplace. For about two weeks every morning when we came down and went into the sitting room we would find one of the pictures turned face down. It was always the same picture; a picture of my gran and grandad. This made me think back to when my sister said that she thought she saw the figure of a man standing in the kitchen of the other house. I asked her if she felt that it could have been Grandad. She did not know as she did not see a face and it was only for a split second that she had seen the man's figure.

As you see, ghosts can follow you.

MARK, COUNTY DUBLIN

While on holiday in County Kerry we stayed in a hotel that had been at one point in its life a grand stately home. I recall one morning I woke up on what would have been a very nice day. As I raised my head to get out of bed, I noticed that there was a woman, completely shrouded in darkness, standing at the foot of our bed. I could tell that she was a woman only by the outline of her body because the rest of her was pitch-black, including her face. I knew that it was not my wife as she was asleep beside me. The woman just stood there, facing in my direction and not saying a word. The first glimpse of her sent me into a paralysed state. I could not even scream out. During that time, I was trying to put myself back together from the shock but I couldn't rationalise what I was seeing.

After some time I managed to turn to my wife and wake her from her sleep. I said to her, 'There is a woman standing at the end of our bed. Well, I think it's a woman.'

'Don't be silly!' she replied. 'Who would be in our room. It's all in your imagination.' My wife took a peek over the bed covers to discover that it was not my imagination. The woman was still standing there. It was then that my wife let out a shout: 'Who are you?' The woman turned, walked over towards the bathroom and vanished. I climbed out of bed and slowly walked across the room towards where she had vanished to check if she was hiding anywhere – but nothing. She was gone. We couldn't rationalise what we had seen, so we decided that we would ask the staff if they knew anything about strange happenings in our room. To our surprise all the staff knew about the strange lady who haunted the hotel. They tried to reassure us that she would not harm us in any way.

This was not our only encounter with the ghostly apparition. On another evening my wife and I were returning to our room after some late-night drinks in the hotel bar. As we reached the top of the stairs to our floor we turned to walk down to our room and there she was, the same figure. She was standing outside one of the rooms. Then she vanished into the room. By this I mean that the door did not open; she just walked through it. We did not sleep a wink that night for wondering if she would ever return. The rest of our stay at the hotel went off with no more sightings of the lady. We did eventually get over the shock of what had happened to us and have stayed there since. Sadly on our second visit we did not see or hear anything of the ghostly lady. We do plan to visit the hotel again.

LILLIAN, DUBLIN

A little over a year ago, my fiancé and I moved into a quiet apartment complex in South Dublin. We loved the apartment from the moment we walked in. It was spacious, with an enormous master bedroom and plenty of closet space. Things were quiet for the first few months, but that changed when I started to notice strange occurrences throughout our home.

The first incident occurred while I was on the computer in the second bedroom. I was typing up a paper when I heard a loud crash coming from the living room. It sounded like the entertainment centre had fallen over and so I ran into the living room to see the damage. When I arrived, nothing had been disturbed and the cat was asleep on the couch; so she evidently had not heard anything. As I was standing in the den, I turned to see a plastic cup in the kitchen lift up off the counter, then fly across the room, hitting the opposite wall. Needless to say, I was pretty scared. I ran back to the second bedroom and shut myself in until my fiancé arrived home from work.

I began to think I was going crazy as I was the only one who witnessed anything strange in the apartment. This changed when my parents came to visit me a month or two ago. My mother was sitting on the couch that faced the kitchen and my dad and I were sitting on the sofa that was against the adjacent wall. Dad and I were discussing my upcoming plans for graduation, when Mum let out an ear-piercing shriek. After we calmed her down, she explained that she had seen a figure all dark and cloud-like come out from around the fridge, then disappear.

Recently, my parents spent the weekend with us again

and slept in the spare room adjacent to ours. My mother was wide-awake, watching television, when at about 2.30 in the morning she felt something move the end of the bed. She thought nothing more of it and promptly fell asleep. It wasn't until the morning that she realised that it must have been the ghost. My mother refuses to sleep in the bedroom again.

I'll be moving soon and I honestly have to say that I will miss this apartment – ghosts and all.

EMILY, COUNTY MEATH

My parents bought the family home just outside Navan, County Meath, in 1969. It sits on about two acres of farmland. Massive trees surround it. It has a big kitchen, dining room and a parlour with a bay window, a bedroom and a bathroom downstairs. The stairs are just off the main entrance hall and lead to the three bedrooms. It is your typical country estate manor house. My brother had already married and had his own family home, not too far from us at this time. My sister Janet and I slept upstairs and my parents slept downstairs.

The strange happenings started slowly, with noises that at first could be explained or shrugged away. As the house is located close to a heavily-used main road, it was easy to blame some strange things on the traffic. Slowly but surely things began to happen that couldn't be explained. I heard my name being called on two occasions. Janet spent only one year in the house before going away to college, leaving me alone upstairs. Sleeping became a challenge.

The most common happening was on the stairs. Footsteps could be heard; something was running up and down the stairs. Whoever it was would not stop. It would run up the stairs, turn and run back down, only to turn around and run back up. This went on all night long. At first, I was terrified! Then I tried to see what was making this noise but every time I stepped outside my bedroom the noise would stop. Then one night I was listening to the running up and down but this time it did not turn and go back down; it continued towards my room. The footsteps continued into my room although the door did not open. I knew I wasn't alone. I could feel a presence in my room. Whatever it was that made the noises on the stairs was now in my room! It paced around. I was frozen with terror. Finally, the pacing stopped and I started screaming! I didn't sleep in my room for weeks after that.

As time went by we kids became adults and went on with our lives. We never ever forget the ghostly happenings of that house. Janet married and had a little boy, Jason. She slept over at the family home with her son on several occasions while her husband was away on business. They stayed in my old room.

One night, Janet was about to fall asleep but in the light from the passing traffic she saw something in the room. She realised she was seeing a thick black cloud enveloping the light from the traffic. She said a prayer and the black cloud left. This 'black cloud' was seen several times. Jason started talking about his playmate upstairs. When questioned, he insisted there was a little girl living in my bedroom!

There are numerous stories about this old house but because Mum and Dad thought we were all nuts, we didn't share our experiences with them. I eventually married and moved to Drogheda. When Mum and Dad reached their mid-sixties, they felt the house was too large for them to look after. They asked if any of us would like to own it but we all said no thanks. So the family home was sold. I often wonder if that ghost still wanders up and down the stairs.

HEATHER, COUNTY DUBLIN

It was either August or September 1972. All I remember for sure was that I was sixteen and my sister was eighteen. My parents looked after an old lady we knew. She lived down the village from us. This lady used to ask my parents if my sister and I could sleep over some time. We did not know why she wanted this – maybe she was just lonely. She lived in an old country mansion that had been converted into an old folks' home. She had a nice two bed-roomed apartment: her own bedroom and the guest room. The guest room was small. There was a double bed with a bedside table and a lamp. There was also an old-style wardrobe. The bed was covered with loads of heavy old blankets and the room generally smelt old. At the end of the bed was a free-standing mirror.

On the night that we slept over I could just not sleep well. I kept on tossing and turning, sometimes dozing off, unlike my sister, who could sleep standing up. I recall that I woke up in the middle of the night and it was very hot. I put this down to the heavy blankets that covered me on the bed. I sat up in the bed to get some air and switched on the table lamp, as I wanted to remove some of the blankets. As I switched on the light I naturally looked around the room but was stunned to see that reflected in the mirror was the image of an old lady with curly white hair. She wore an old-fashioned dress with an apron tied around her waist.

She seemed to be looking for something in the room. Yet she was not in the room. Then the lady stopped and looked straight at me. I can still see her eyes gazing into mine. She smiled at me, then vanished.

I shot under the blankets and stayed there. I left the light on for the rest of the night. I know that it was not a dream because I was scared out of my wits. The next morning we stayed with the old lady until our mother collected us. But I could not leave it at that. I had to know what I saw in the bedroom that night. I pretended that I had left something behind so as I could run back to the old lady's house. I did not know how I was going to ask her about what I saw. But as I sat beside her I blurted out, 'Do you have a ghost in your second bedroom? I saw something last night.' The old lady chuckled and gave a huge smile. 'Oh you see her too. That is the spirit of a woman who lived here long before it became an old folks' home. She has been seen in several parts of the house. I think she has lost something of great importance as she is always looking for something.'

I recall the old lady patting me on the head and smiling. 'Run along, child. Your mother will be wondering where you are.' I became a regular visitor to the old lady but never saw the ghost again. I have often wondered who she was and what she had lost. Will she ever find it, find peace and be able to pass on fully?

MAURA, WICKLOW TOWN

I was seventeen when my best friend Alison, also seventeen, committed suicide. I had seen her the night she died. She was over at my house and we were up in my room. We were talking about how happy she was in her current relationship and other girly stuff. She didn't mention anything out of the ordinary or give any sign that she was depressed in any way. She then left to go to her boyfriend's house. The next morning, my phone rang. It was Alison's mother in hysterics. She told me Alison had hanged herself in her bedroom. I couldn't believe it!

One week later I was at her funeral. So many people turned up; the whole town loved her. I cried the whole day. I still couldn't believe she was gone. I wanted to go in and see Alison as she lay in her coffin, to say goodbye. I made it as far as the door, but I couldn't face her. I broke down before I could do it. I felt terrible guilt for not going in to see her for the very last time.

That night I was lying in the dark in my bed. It was around 1.30 am and I couldn't sleep. Suddenly I felt the sensation of something or someone sitting on the end of my bed. I sat up to look. At first I did not know what was going on; my heart was racing in my chest. Sitting on my bed was Alison. She smiled at me and whispered, 'Don't worry, everything will be all right now.'

For some reason I started talking back even though I knew Alison was dead. 'Why did you do it?' I asked.

'I could not live with the shame,' she replied.

'The shame of what?' I asked.

'Being pregnant,' she replied. I had no idea she was pregnant. 'I am OK now,' she said. 'Tell Mam I'm sorry. Tell her I am so sorry.'

Then Alison left as suddenly as she had appeared. The weight that I felt on my bed lifted; she was gone. The next day, with tears in my eyes, I went to see Alison's mother. We chatted for a while, then I told her that I had seen Alison in my room the previous night. She looked at me as if I had two heads. I told her what Alison had said about being pregnant. With that she broke down in tears. Not even her parents knew. They found out the truth only from the post-mortem. We spent the rest of the day talking about Alison and how much we both would miss her. I still miss her and I always will. I wish she were still here.

MARY, COUNTY DUBLIN

My story begins in 1999 when I was sixteen years old. I am originally from Wexford but am living in Lucan now. I was sitting with my friend in her bedroom doing the usual teenage girl thing; giggling, talking and munching junk food. All of a sudden, we heard the front door open and slam and it sounded as if someone was stomping through the living room and into the kitchen. My friend looked surprised at this as she was not expecting anyone home. She left the room to go and investigate this but returned even more surprised as she found nobody else in the house and the front and back doors were locked. We had both heard the noises so it could not have been our imagination. Several minutes later we heard the stomping again. I was by now terrified. I didn't consider this to be a paranormal event at the time because before this nothing weird had happened to me. It was quite a while before we were brave enough to venture into the living room and, to our relief, there was no one there.

From that point on, my own house (not my friend's house, where it all started) became a hub of paranormal activity. All sorts of things happened, from electrical appliances acting up to voices being heard and even wall markings. My family and friends can bear witness to this unexpected guest moving in. The doorbell would ring and when we went to answer the door no one was there. This has been going on since that time I stayed over at my friend's house. The degree of activity would increase and decrease without any kind of consistency. One thing remained constant; marks would appear on the walls regardless of where I lived.

Activity also continues at my old home in Wexford but nothing like the activity at my home in Swords. The most drastic event I've personally experienced was when a glass that was sitting on my sink moved. It just slid straight across the sink for no apparent reason. Our pets have problems as well. Our cats chase something I cannot see all over the house. The family dog back home is also known for barking madly at walls. To date whatever it is that haunts me (and I feel it is me as it seems to follow me everywhere I go) has not harmed me in any way, just given me the odd fright every now and again. I wish I could find out who or what it is that haunts me. I feel it may be an old family member who is upset over something in the past.

FRANCES, COUNTY CORK

My husband Tom and our children and I moved to Dublin in 1994, when he was promoted at work and made head of the Dublin branch of his company. Our lives were generally quiet until 2001, when Tom died suddenly of a massive heart attack. It came as a great shock to the family as we had no idea that he had any heart problems. We did know that it ran in his family but somehow always hoped it would spare him. In the days after his death I wasn't sleeping well. One night exhaustion finally took over and I fell into a deep sleep. Incredibly, I recall waking up to see Tom walking into the bedroom and sitting down beside me. I was frozen to the spot. I knew Tom was dead but I knew it was he who was sitting there. As you may imagine, I was astonished because I realised he wasn't alive. We chatted for a short while. Tom told me that he was fine and that I needed to carry on with my life, to take care of our two sons who were still at home, who at the time were twelve and sixteen. Then he stood up, said goodbye and left. As you can imagine this broke my heart. It was like going through the whole grieving process again.

That night has stayed in my memory and always will. This was my first experience with the spirit of my husband Tom, but not my last. Years passed and my sons and I moved back to Cork. Some time later I developed arthritis. The weather in Cork was always cold and damp and it aggravated my arthritis so I decided to move back to Dublin. Work was difficult and painful for me because of the arthritis but I managed to work for many years. One evening after work I came home, lay on the sofa after I had something to eat and turned on the television. Although pain had now become my constant companion, on this day it was far worse. Pain was shooting down both arms and also radiating from the chest area just below my rib cage. I remember thinking I could not take this pain any more. I was almost at the end of my tether.

Feeling exhausted was normal for me so I decided to take a couple of aspirin and stretch out on the sofa for a few minutes. Then the most amazing thing happened. My husband Tom came into the room and sat down beside me.

I recall that a feeling of warmth and care came over me but I knew that he was no longer living. At the same time, I noticed that my pain was disappearing. My husband and I talked for a few minutes and I began to feel healthy, just as I had when Tom and I first met. I suddenly blurted out, 'I want to go with you, Tom. I am so tired. I need to rest.' Tom looked at me hard and answered a firm, 'No. You can't come with me. You must remain here. Not for a long time yet can you come with me.' Then he stood up. He said that he had to go but asked me to keep my mobile phone close to me over the next few days as I might need it in an emergency. He smiled at me and left.

Later on that week I felt what I thought was my arthritis pain coming back but quickly realised that this was something else altogether. I could feel pains running down my arms. The pain in the rib cage was overwhelming. I grabbed my mobile and rang for an ambulance. I was rushed to the hospital. I was having a heart attack. My heart stopped beating while I was in hospital and twice had to be restarted by electric shock.

I recovered from my ordeal and was released from hospital. I believe that my husband visited me not just to comfort me in a time of need but to warn me about what was about to happen. So if you ever get a visit from a departed loved one, keep in mind that it may be a message or warning. Try very hard to decipher any messages they might bring. I do miss Tom but I am happy that he is still there watching over me. I also know that he will come to collect me when it is my time to pass over.

NICOLA, DUBLIN

For several years, my family and I have realised that our house, which we've lived in for nearly eight years, is haunted. We live in Dundrum in Dublin. Our house doesn't appear to be out of the ordinary in any way. It is located in the older section of Dundrum and, although I do not know the exact date of construction, I think that it was most likely built some time in the 1970s or 1980s, as it is typical Dublin Corporation in design. To the best of our knowledge, nobody has died in the house. However, somebody still resides here alongside my family.

About two or three years ago, I tended to stay awake much later than the rest of my family and I'd sit downstairs and watch television. Every night at around 1 am I would see a shadow move along the banister upstairs. More recently, I haven't stayed up so late. Even though I don't see the shadow any more, my dad has occasionally spoken of seeing something moving upstairs while he watches television.

Last year, I was watching television late into the night, when out of the corner of my eye I saw a person sitting on the stairs. I turned and the person remained long enough for me to notice that it was the figure of a young woman. She was looking down at the floor so I could not see her face as it was covered by her hair. She was wearing a blue skirt and matching top. I was drinking a cup of tea at the time. I turned to put it down and go to investigate who this was but when I looked back around she was gone.

You might think my reaction to seeing someone sitting on our stairs strange and calm. This is because after experiencing her in our home for such a long time we somehow regard her as part of the family. We have decided not to give her a name as we feel this would be disrespectful to her real name, whatever that is. One day, my mum was talking to me in the kitchen about my college grades, when we heard the front door open and a person run up the stairs. We both assumed that my brother had come home early, so my mum went up into his room to see why he was home from school so early but he wasn't there. Nobody else was upstairs. As she was coming back down the stairs she called me out to the stairs. 'Can you smell that?' she asked me and I said I could. I distinctly smelled perfume on the stairs.

Just a few weeks ago, my mum came running upstairs to wake me up so that I could get ready for college, only to find me ready. She was glad that I had woken by myself but I explained to her that she had called me by name to get me up much earlier. She denied ever calling me. I can only assume it was our female guest from the stairs.

Most recently, I was outside with some friends playing soccer in the backyard after dark when one of them said, 'When I smelled cigarette smoke and saw a shadow on the fence, I looked and saw your mum up in your room looking down at us.' As I turned to look I could see my mum sitting in the front room watching television. I glanced up at my room and, yes, I could see the figure of a woman looking out my window. I pretended to my friends that it was my aunt upstairs in case they saw my mum in the front room as well. We are a very spiritual family and have never felt in any way afraid or in danger as a result of our visitor. Or are we visitors in *her* home? We feel very special that she has chosen to show herself to us. This might sound a little strange but I would miss her should she decide not to visit any more.

ALISON, COUNTY DUBLIN

It was on 12 March 2004 that my boyfriend and best friend committed suicide. It was as if as if someone put a hand into my chest and ripped out my heart. I felt as if my life had ended also. I had no idea that Liam was suffering from depression and was finding his studies difficult. Liam's suicide was a total shock for all us. After his death I didn't spend time with my other friends. I spent a lot of time alone in my college dormitory trying to come to terms with Liam's death. My other college friends were all getting on with their lives and letting me do my grief thing. I did most of my homework in my room, as my teachers gave me a week off in order to collect myself.

One afternoon after lunch I went into my room to check my email. I was alone in the apartment; my roommates were in class. I sat down at the computer and started crying. I just didn't want to be alone at this point and I was really missing Liam. It just didn't feel right. I got it together and started typing an email to my parents back home to tell them that I would be coming home for the weekend. My mind was clear when all a sudden I felt a presence behind me. The sensation was so strong. It was as if someone was brushing up against my back a little. I turned around quickly. Nothing. I could still feel the presence, though. You know how you can just tell if someone's in a house or a room with you? So I walked around the apartment to check if any of my roommates had returned from lectures. No one was there.

I sat back down at the computer and started typing again. The presence was still really strong. After a couple of minutes, I felt as though an invisible person was embracing me from behind. Something brushed against both of my arms, like someone rubbing them from behind. I could feel my heart pounding in my chest, yet I knew deep down inside that whoever this was meant me no harm. Then what felt like two cool fingers brushed against the right side of my face. I knew it was Liam. I could totally feel his presence. He hugged me, rubbed my arms and touched my face. I just knew it. I began to cry. I turned around, just knowing I would see him there. Nothing. I could feel his presence stronger than ever as I turned back, hoping to catch a glimpse of him, but after about ten seconds, he was gone.

It was a truly incredible experience, an experience that I know will stay with me forever. When I tell people about it, they believe me! Or they pretend to, at least. Other friends who knew Liam have had similar experiences with a presence they thought was him, but not quite as physical. They felt more of the presence than the actual touching. I discussed my experience with Liam's parents. His mother told me that one night just before she fell asleep in bed she thought she felt a hand rubbing her head as she nodded off but dismissed it as her imagination. Now she believes it was her son Liam saying goodnight. I have not felt Liam's presence around me again as strongly as I did that night but I know he is always looking after me and his loved ones.

SEAN, COUNTY CORK

It was in 1997 that I inherited my grandparents' home. I had moved out of my family home when I was a young man of eighteen and wanted to discover the world. I met my wife and lived in an apartment in Dublin. It was after my grandmother's death that I inherited her home. It was left to my parents but they had a home of their own and asked me if I would like it. I discussed this with my wife who after some consideration decided that this might just be a new start as things where not going as we had planned in Dublin. So in August of 1997 we moved into Grandma's house in Cobh. Everything was going great for us. I had a new job and my wife was expecting our first child. It was during this time that strange things began to happen.

At first it was just my wife who began to experience them. She would wake in the middle of the night to the sound of a baby crying. Then I began to hear it. We enquired of our neighbours on each side of us if they had a child staying with them; neither of them did. Then we saw her. One night my wife woke me from my sleep. 'Do you hear that?' she asked. I listened closely. I could hear a baby crying, not from outside but from inside our home. We got up to investigate. As we opened our bedroom door both my wife and I saw what we believe to be a ghost. We saw a figure of an old lady on our stairs. She was dressed in Victorian clothing and seemed to be looking for something. She went down the stairs and into the living room. I sent my wife back into the bedroom as I rushed downstairs to see who this was. I called out, 'Who are you?' But as I followed her into the living room she vanished. I must add that all the doors and windows of the house were locked so she could not have escaped from the house; yet she was gone.

Perplexed by this, I asked my parents the next day if either of them had ever heard anything about what we had just experienced. I could tell that they had. So I asked them to tell all. They went on to tell of a similar incident experienced by my grandparents when they were expecting their children. My mother said, 'It was only while your grandmother was pregnant that these things happened. They reported that they would hear and experience exactly what you have described. On one occasion in the middle of the night, they also heard the crying. Your grandfather got out of bed and saw the figure of a ghostly woman going down the stairs.' They explained that in the late eighteen hundreds a woman who lived in that house gave birth to a stillborn child and died herself shortly after the birth. My parents said they believed that any time a woman was pregnant in the house that spirit of the woman returned to look for the baby from which she was separated in childbirth.

Hearing this tragic story did not make us feel any better about staying in the house. We began to search for a new home and sold up. We now live in a newly built ghost-free house. We have a beautiful daughter and things are really looking up for us. I often think about my gran's house and wonder if the old woman will ever find her lost child.

GRACE, COUNTY DOWN

It was while both my husband and I were on holiday in County Kerry that we had our first and only paranormal experience. We stayed in an old hotel in Killarney. Our bedroom was in a very nice suite. Initially, I was unaware of any strange activity in the room but during the evening I became aware of a moving shadowy figure, and at times two figures, from the corner of my right eye on the wall to the right of me. At first I thought it was the flickering of the television reflected on the wall. However, when I looked directly at the shadows, there was never anything visible. At times while watching television at night, I observed a streak of light shooting across the sitting room of the hotel suite. My husband never saw any of this. Several times when the shadowy figures were visible from the corner of my eye, I would alert my husband without looking at them but he couldn't see anything.

One night, at about 11.30, I was watching television with my husband after a meal and a few drinks in the hotel bar. During the commercial break I popped into the bathroom. The bathroom door was ajar so I didn't need to switch on the light as the light from the bedroom lit up the bathroom and as we were the only guests staying in the suite I felt no need to lock the door. I heard footsteps from the other room coming towards the bathroom. They were the sounds of footsteps on a wooden floor, yet all the rooms, apart from the bathroom which had marble tiles, had heavy carpet. The person following me obscured the stream of light which spilt into the bathroom for a moment before moving into the bedroom. I assumed it was my husband as there was no one else with us. Moments later, I looked into the bedroom but my husband wasn't in there. I was surprised as the person hadn't returned to the other room of the suite. So I popped into the sitting room and my husband was still sitting in his chair with his feet up, reading his book. He confirmed that he hadn't moved at all.

Sometimes I was followed into the bedroom by this shadow and at times there would be a marked change in the temperature from normal to very cold. Oddly, only I experienced this and only I was aware of the footsteps and observed the shadow following me.

The next night, I woke up in the early hours of the morning for no apparent reason. My husband was sound asleep (the bedroom was not at all dark) and my eyes were drawn toward the open bedroom door. Suddenly at the doorway appeared a young man in his early twenties with dark hair, blue eyes, slim build and wearing a light-blue, long-sleeved jumper. I violently shook my husband, who woke, shouting, 'What's wrong?'

I said, 'There is a man in our room.'

My husband was staring at the end of our bed as this young man passed, looking at us with the most beautiful smile. He lifted his right hand, as if apologetically, in greeting. I assumed he was apologising for intruding on us in our bedroom. He continued across the room from the right of the bed to the left side, walked straight through the wall into the adjoining room and disappeared. My husband and I jumped up out of our bed and got dressed. We went straight down to reception where we explained to the receptionist what we had just witnessed. She gave us a puzzled look but could clearly see we were distressed. She gave us another room and had our personal belongings brought to the other room as neither of us wanted to go back into the original room again.

I was really taken aback and didn't know what to make

of it. I lay awake for a couple of hours, wondering what we had just witnessed. I was aware of some presence in the hotel room. The next morning the manager of the hotel approached us and apologised for our experience. He told us that other guests had seen this young man in the same suite as us. He asked us to tell him our story for his records and reassured us that at no time over the many years had anyone ever been harmed by this spirit. He believed the figure to be the spirit of one of the people who had owned the building before it became a hotel. He was killed in a car crash. Research was carried out and it was discovered that the wall between our suite and the other room passes through what would have been his old bedroom. Thankfully we did not have any more night-time visits from the spirit and we did receive a discount from the hotel for our unexpected guest.

NOEL, DUBLIN

I am sixty-seven years old and up until recently I was employed by the Irish Prison Service. I am now retired from the prison service and enjoying retirement. Some years ago I was on duty in one of Dublin city prisons. It was about 4 am and I was doing my routine patrols of the landings. As I approached the clock where we do our half-hour check I saw a figure of what I can only describe as an old prison officer dressed in a very old-fashioned prison officer's uniform. At first I thought it was another officer playing a prank on me as we all knew the story of the prison ghost but when I approached this figure it just vanished. When I returned to the duty room I told my colleagues what I had witnessed. Several of them went to the area to see if they could see the figure for themselves.

On another occasion I was on an exterior patrol. I approached a gate that I needed to pass through. I took my keys from my pocket and placed the appropriate key into the gate lock. As I did I looked to my left and towards the corner of the wall which was approximately a hundred yards away. As I looked I saw a dark shadow-like figure, of a male about six feet tall. I saw this figure pass through a gate without opening it and walk down towards the back of the canteen area. I immediately radioed to my colleagues that someone was in the area. A thorough search of the area was carried out but nothing was found except the locked gate.

The next day I attended work and spoke to my boss about what I had seen. His immediate reaction was to say, 'Oh my God! You have just made the hairs stand up on the back of my neck. I know that what you are saying is true because I have already had so many reports of the same thing you describe from staff, prisoners and, in particular, night staff.'

Since then several members of staff have said to me that they saw the same thing. Not all prison officers have seen the ghost. It's strange that it is a mix of old and new officers who see him – you would think that it would only be the senior staff members.

In another prison not too far from where I served, prison officers have reported seeing similar things, especially in and around the area of the hanging cell where a ghostly figure of an old prison officer has also been seen.

Conclusion

As Ireland's leading paranormal investigator I am always asked one question, 'Are you ever afraid of ghosts?'

I always give the same answer, 'No, I am more afraid of my wife.'

As funny as this reply may sound, it holds some truth. Ghosts, spirits or poltergeists – put whatever title on them you will – can never at any time harm you. They can never have the level of energy that you as a living person possess. For them to manifest or even come into our environment they must draw from our energy or from the energy of electronic devices around us and they can never possess more energy than us. So please don't fear them but try to communicate with them as they have made a huge effort to get back here. At least say, 'Hi!' Also remember that they, at some time, were living beings, maybe your own distant relatives. Maybe you are now living in the house they once lived in. So at all times please show them the respect they deserve.

May God's love shine on you and guide you through life.

Paul Fennell, October 2009